A SCRAP
IN THE
BLESSINGS
JAR

SOUTHERN MESSENGER POETS

Dave Smith, Series Editor

Also by David Bottoms

NEW AND SELECTED POEMS

A SCRAP IN THE BLESSINGS JAR

DAVID BOTTOMS

Edited, with an Introduction, by ERNEST SUAREZ

Louisiana State University Press   Baton Rouge

Published by Louisiana State University Press
lsupress.org

Manufactured in the United States of America
First printing

Designer: Barbara Neely Bourgoyne
Typefaces: Minion Pro and Requiem
Printer and binder: Sheridan Books

Cover image copyright © Curt Richter Photography.

Library of Congress Cataloging-in-Publication Data
Names: Bottoms, David, author. | Suarez, Ernest, editor, writer of
    introduction.
Title: A scrap in the blessings jar : new and selected poems / David
    Bottoms ; edited, with an introduction, by Ernest Suarez.
Description: Baton Rouge : Louisiana State University Press, [2023] |
    Series: Southern Messenger Poets
Identifiers: LCCN 2023012361 (print) | LCCN 2023012362 (ebook) |
    ISBN 978-0-8071-8069-3 (cloth) | ISBN 978-0-8071-8031-0 (paperback) |
    ISBN 978-0-8071-8076-1 (pdf) | ISBN 978-0-8071-8075-4 (epub)
Subjects: LCGFT: Poetry.
Classification: LCC PS3552.O819 S37 2023 (print) | LCC PS3552.O819
    (ebook) | DDC 811/.5/4—dc23/eng/20230316
LC record available at https://lccn.loc.gov/2023012361
LC ebook record available at https://lccn.loc.gov/2023012362

This book, and everything else, is

for Kelly and Rachel and Wren

CONTENTS

INTRODUCTION

David Bottoms was among the generation of southern poets who followed Robert Penn Warren and James Dickey. Like them, he was a story-teller whose work often explored the tensions between the self, society, and nature. Unlike them, he embraced the possibility of religious belief. Where Warren was an uneasy skeptic, and Dickey was an existentialist who thought that no moral force governed the universe, Bottoms was a Christian, part of Flannery O'Connor's "Christ-haunted South," though not conventionally or unquestioningly. At times he stared into "the darkness we're all headed for" ("Shooting Rats at the Bibb County Dump") and at other times discovered "mercy enough to consume us all and give us wings" ("Under the Vulture-Tree"). His remarks to students suggest his larger aim:

> . . . the first thing I say to people who come into my introductory class . . . is something like this: "It's nice if you know what a dactyl is, or an anapest, or if you know what a sonnet is. That's nice, but that's not the most important thing. Not by a long shot. If you only learn one thing in this class, I want you to learn how to use language to get at what's important to you in your life." That's what I'm about. Learn how to use language to get at what's important to you in your life.[1]

Bottoms spent most of his life in Georgia. He was born in Canton in 1949 and died in Atlanta in the spring of 2023. He graduated from Mercer University in Macon in 1971 and began publishing poetry in magazines and journals, drawing on Macon for settings that range from Rose Hill Cemetery, to the infamous Sunshine Club, to the local VFW. In 1979 he was teaching high school in Douglas County when Warren selected his manuscript as the winner of the Walt Whitman Award, a first book competition sponsored by the Academy of American Poets. He then entered the Ph.D. program at Florida State University in Tallahassee, a city whose rivers and swampy outskirts provided additional settings for his early poems. After finishing the degree in 1982, he joined the English Department at Georgia State University in Atlanta, where he taught until his retirement in 2020. His poems began to depict life in the Atlanta area, especially the suburban experiences of a man newly married and a father, a world different from the wild creatures and environments of his earlier poems, but where snakes, turtles, birds, insects, and an occasional fox maintain a stealthy presence.

Poetry served as Bottoms's vehicle to conduct spiritual travel between these worlds, often in a manner noticeably akin to the traditional quest journey. From 1980 to 2018 he published eight books of poetry—the last four by Copper Canyon Press—that gradually became more overtly metaphysical. In these books, and the new poems in this volume, his subject matter—the woods, animals, family, fishing, sports, music—remained consistent, but his techniques shifted as his spiritual quest evolved. In his citation for the 1979 Walt Whitman award, Warren noted that "much of" Bottoms's "strength emerges from the fact that he is temperamentally a realist. In his vision the actual world is not transformed but illuminated."[2] By 2021 Edward Hirsch described him as a "poet of idiomatic eloquence" whose later work takes on the qualities of "weighty late devotionals—psychical, otherworldly."[3]

This book isn't a collection of new and finest poems, but a gathering of representative works. Bottoms's poetry can be divided into three relatively distinct phases. *Shooting Rats at the Bibb County Dump* (1980) and his next three books consist of compact, country narratives meant to reveal "something about the hidden things of the world. The vague or shadowy relationships and connections that exist just below the surface of our daily lives."[4] Here his language is figurative and naturalistic. The poems are often characterized by epiphanies, moments of revelation, sometimes expressed in a single line, that simultaneously amplify and focus the poem. In "Sign for My Father, Who Stressed the Bunt"—one of his many poems involving boyhood and baseball—the narrator recalls practicing with his father, who emphasized the bunt while the narrator wanted to hit homeruns. The poem concludes with a series of metaphors that are illuminated by the last line:

> That whole tiresome pitch
> About basics never changing,
> and I never learned what you were laying down.

Like a hand brushed across the bill of a cap,
let this be the sign
I'm getting a grip on the sacrifice.

Other poems draw on archetypal patterns. "Under the Boathouse" emphasizes "submersion, symbolic death, ascension, and rebirth."[5] In the poem a man leaps off a diving board, snares the palm of his hand on a large hook someone has left in the water, and finds himself caught "halfway between the bottom of the lake / and the bottom of the sky." Almost of out of breath, he sees his wife's "shadow like an angel" quiver on the surface, pulls free, and surfaces with a new sense of the liminal space between life and the afterlife.

After the publication of *Armored Hearts: Selected and New Poems* (1996), Bottoms began composing longer, looser conversational poems that move from a more traditional line to a balanced or split line. The poems of his middle period—*Vagrant Grace* (1999) and *Waltzing through the Endtime* (2004)—often center on events and regrets that prick his narrators' memories and wend towards small and large revelations, the discovery of the extraordinary in the ordinary. The shift to longer, Charles Wright–like structures is an attempt to find a convincing foundation and platform for his metaphysical beliefs. While Warren's self-explorations halted at transcendental yearnings, and Dickey fashioned dramatic narratives that emphasized existential acts or "creative lies," Wright, ultimately a secular poet, created meditative structures, which Bottoms adapted. In "Country Store and Moment of Grace," Bottoms describes his aesthetic: the narrator attempts to arrange "memory / these little scraps of consequence" at a time in life when "memory becomes portentous, / like some newfound gospel / promising, finally, the whole fantastic story / and unscrolling into fragments." The narrator realizes that the relationship between past and recent memories, and "grace" can be "vagrant," wayward, associational, and altering. In contrast to his early poetry's stress on epiphanies and archetypal patterns, in these poems insight results from personal memories that accrue—sometimes unsteadily and perhaps unreliably—and shape the past towards significance. The poems of this period are also more straightforwardly biographical. His wife, Kelly, and his daughter, Rachel, are more present. His relationship with his father and mother, his childhood and adolescence in Georgia, in the segregated South, and the Baptist religion of his youth are detailed more intimately. He enters into the familiarity of dialogue with his reader, at times evoking what in "Night Strategies" he calls "this nervous / exaggeration of tenderness."

The new poems in this volume, written under the duress of significant illness, and the poems from his two previous books—*We Almost Disappear* (2011), *Otherworld, Underworld, Prayer Porch* (2018)—are composed in shorter formats resembling his earlier books, but retain the associative, ruminative qualities of his middle period. They are meditative, personal, unfolding from the perspective of an older man surveying life, someone who has been long-married, experienced raising a daughter, and tended to a dying father and mother. They look backward for some consolation, for glimpses of truth. In a new poem, "A Scrap in the Blessings Jar," the narrator is at home, content and alone, when "Suddenly, it seemed, I needed nothing," a blessing that results in a poem. He places the poem where it will touch his family, and by extension, the reader:

> I wrote this on a scrap of paper and dropped it
> into our blessings jar.

Other late poems invoke darkness, stillness, silences, and absences, but without ennui or despair. For David Bottoms poetry can provide understanding, at times a tone of celebration, a sense of discovery, spiritual possibilities, and meaning. The conclusion of "A Scrawny Fox"—the final poem in *Otherworld*—is evocative, representative, and telling:

> Maybe you tire and close your eyes. Things happen
> when you close your eyes—an owl leaves a branch trembling,
>
> the dog food disappears. You'd love to see that fox again.
> Near the end, though, only one thing matters,
>
> And nothing, not even the fox, moves as quietly.

NOTES

    1. "A Conversation with David Bottoms, Rattle #39, Spring 2013, https://www.rattle.com /a-conversation-with-david-bottoms/ (retrieved 6/26/2022).

    2. "Publishing: Georgian, 29, Wins Poetry Award," Thomas Lask, *New York Times,* April 20, 1979, Section C, p. 28.

3. Edward Hirsch, "On David Bottoms: Hymns to the Unknown," *Literary Matters,* issue 13.3, Spring/Summer 2021 (https://www.literarymatters.org/13-3-on-david-bottoms-hymns-to-the-unknown/).

4. "David Bottoms," *Southbound: Interviews with Southern Poets,* ed. Ernest Suarez (Columbia: University of Missouri Press, 1999), p. 90.

5. Ibid, 91–92.

NEW POEMS

A SCRAP IN THE BLESSINGS JAR

after Miłosz

For once, the dog was content to snooze under Kelly's piano,
and leaf blowers and lawn mowers rested

in garages and basements. All the wars were on the other side
of the world, every hunger behind me.

Bright sun streaked through backyard pines,
winds gone quiet. I watched a while

from the kitchen window, then read a lovely story by Andre Dubus
and thought of my own daughter sleeping all day

in another city and of my wife away at school
happy to be writing and studying again.

Suddenly, it seemed, I needed nothing.

I wrote this on a scrap of paper and dropped it
into our blessings jar.

WOOD SHOP

When a girl in our school lost a finger in Wood Shop,
Mr. Cline cut from a stray pine board
what he sometimes called a prod, sometimes a handle.
No longer would a student in his shop class
push by hand
any board through a circular saw.

When I spoke of the lost finger to my cousin,
he asked me what she was doing taking Wood Shop.
This was still the sixties
and a girl in shop was way beyond him.

I presumed she was trying to make a point.
What point, he said,
that women could lose fingers too?

That year I kept all of my mine and graduated
with a pine bookcase, badly sanded,
that wobbled on its legs.

Sometimes I remember a high school geometry class,
a girl in a front row desk,
her ring finger bandaged with gauze.

How determined she looked chewing her pencil,
the intricate proofs
of Pythagoras
unraveling behind her eyes.

GRACE

for Martin Bresnick

The old hymn had it right.

I heard it once in my uncle's voice,
risen from an island in the south Pacific
to ride a troop ship into the pulpit of Riverdale Baptist.
I heard it in his voice
a crackling urgency like a potbellied stove,
red and sizzling.
Even from the back pew, you could feel the heat.

I listened all my boyhood,
but my listening couldn't save me.

Maybe you've walked, too, on a Sunday
through your favorite woods
and heard through a distant shuffling of leaves
the far-away rustle of tongues,
the handclapping and tapping of feet,
or the single anguished voice bellowing over a thunder of fans,
and maybe, like me, you've paused in the dogwoods
at the edge of a churchyard
to hear those many tongues twisting into one tongue
around that old hymn
and felt yourself listening suddenly
with your heart.

That wasn't grace, but grace had been there,
the way the stirring of leaves
is not the wind, or the paw print beside the creek
not the fox.

MAINTENANCE

for Louis Corrigan

When my old man died, he left me a truck,
a Chevy Blazer, old but cared for. I gave it to a cousin
because he often sat with my dad

and sometimes stayed overnight
when he was old and sick, and I couldn't get there.
A week or so later, another cousin called and offered

to buy the truck for her father, who was broke
and needed wheels to get to a new job. Often, he and my dad
had changed the oil and filters, and done routine work

on the brakes. But I'd already given the Blazer away.
This uncle was a man I loved. He and my dad
were tight. I felt terrible—

two deserving men and one truck.
"Maintenance is the life
of a truck," my old man would say

as he drove it onto the steel lifts,
and my uncle shoved a spout
into an oil can. Not bad advice

from a man who would never see a doctor
and died a slow and agonizing death
from leukemia.

A SCAR

My cousin could work wonders with his hands.

For his ninth merit badge he carved a lovely neckerchief slide,
the head of an eagle.

I wanted to do as much. I wanted to accomplish something
that someone held in high esteem. What was the truth

about my talents? I sawed a block
from a two-by-four found leaning in a corner of my grandpa's garage,

and borrowed my father's knife,
a Boker Tree Brand, short blade honed to a razor.

I was thinking owl, something mysterious, mystical, something
to express my spiritual side,

but the bird would not rise out of the pine.

I struggled with the beak, with an eye,
but the owl would not rise.

After a short while,
I saw the bloody truth. I'd cut to the bone.

MY FATHER'S VOICE

On the front porch of my grandfather's grocery, in a roll
of fence wire taller than my head,
I was in the calaboose.
My cousin was the sheriff
who'd locked me up. I was five years old. I felt nothing,
but looked down to see a wire running all the way
through my calf. It frightened me.

Next thing I knew my father had a pair of pliers
and was pulling the wire back through my leg.
I remember no blood.

And remember no hospital or tetanus shot,
though I'm sure they were both
part of the day,
only a pair of battery-powered walkie-talkies
(a gift against my pain)
we played with that evening
among the lightning bugs in my grandfather's yard,

and the voice of my father breaking up
and trembling, breaking up
and still trembling
through that cheap tin speaker.

SILENCE AND SOUTHERN MEN

Everything necessary was there—

the soft drink cooler, the straight-backed chairs, the potbelly stove—
but rarely did a story unravel among that circle of men.

In my grandfather's store
silence was the mark of a real man.

Besides, the war had been over for a decade.

Mostly the talk was money, the price of gas and kerosene,
of horse feed or dog chow.

Complaints about the government were a given.
And to speak about something was thought to lessen it.

Speech simply wasn't the currency,

though occasionally, out of some great need, the size of a buck
crept into the crowd,

prompting someone to rise from his chair, lever
the stove door, and spit into the fire.

BACKING UP THE GOSPEL SINGERS

Pickens County, Georgia

A loose hand-clapping
shivers through the crowd, and the gospel singer chords his guitar,
clears his throat, tips the ratty brim of his hat.
He taps the mic, and the tuning drags on behind him—
the banjo, the dobro,
my mandolin—while the low moon in the tent flap settles
on the fiddler's shoulder.

His teenage daughter—or wife—eyes bruised with shadow, hovers
near the bass toward the back of the stage.
The roses on her blousy dress
glow like drops of blood.
                              When the song kicks off,
she lowers her head, and won't meet anyone
eye to eye, not me, the bass player, the banjo player,
not one face in the congregation
scattered in lawn chairs across the sawdust—
as though to say every nerve, trembling and high-strung,
isn't set trembling by the Spirit.

But now his shoulders have caught the beat,
his blue-jeaned hips, the silver toe of his boot,
and when the chorus
comes around and he glances back
for harmony,
                  she watches his hand flap toward the roof,
big hand she saw, only an hour ago, thumbing
a King James under a lantern,

and inches forward, easy, edging
under that hand, his anointed inscrutable hand,
remembering, I imagine,
how quickly it becomes a fist.

LEAF-SCUM

We are all going into a world of dark.
—CHARLES WRIGHT

Thirty-five days without rain and a dingy leaf-scum coats the pond.

Algae thickens in the coves, the creeks dry and leafy and twig-veined.
The pond is down three feet,

and fingerlings no longer dart in the shallows. Mud on mud.

I run a finger along the edge
of a rusty leaf,

and brittle leaves crunch under Jack's paws.

A vague smoke from the burning mountains, miles away,
hangs like sour breath in the trees.

Like everything else, the spirit is dry and sour.

I step toward the path, but Jack
hangs back.

He noses the shadows.

A single water lily floats in the cove,
near twilight the petals are black, the leaf-pads black.

LITTLE DREAM UNDER A WIZARD'S CAP

Like a tune you can't get out of your head—say "That Old Black Magic"
or "The Bear Went Over the Mountain"—

a stone tower keeps rising by the bruised lake of my sleep, and sure enough,
I'm climbing those spiral steps again
                                   into that upper room
where out of the clotted darkness
gray and portly oaks stretch their arms toward the windows.

Space for the spaceless kingdom, Jung called his tower in Bollingen . . .
closets enough for all the conundrums
of the psyche—
                 which doesn't clear much mist off my dream path
through the forest, or unravel this chronic prowling
among antique books and maps.

Maybe you, too, believe the world is always intimating secrets,
both worlds, and have taken

to consulting seers, reading the tarot,
even sleeping in a nightcap

sprinkled with crescents and stars.

LITTLE NIGHT OWL

For hours I'd lug her on my shoulder,
up and down the sidewalk in front of that crumbling pre-war two-story

where we lived under the tap shoes
of a struggling hoofer. Up and down that sidewalk, stumbling

over cracks, singing those flies off the buttermilk, that bear
over the mountain,

and often saw the sun peep up over the rooftops of the renovated cottages
on Ridgeway. The child just wasn't a sleeper.

This song, that song, this shoulder, that shoulder,
and the girl wouldn't nod. Nothing to do—

just night after night, up and down the sidewalk, staggering
in a trance of exhaustion, bouncing

that swaddled grumbler, night after night of the moon
climbing through stars

while one by one the houses closed their weepy lids
and the street lamps flung our shadows

in front of us, then behind us, then in front of us again,
until I'd paced the whole block I don't know

how many times until the worn-out moon started to fade
like a marshmallow in a cup of hot chocolate

and I'm dodging a car groaning out of a driveway,
a flying newspaper, the rolling

stench of a garbage truck. Then it hits me
the kid's not stirring, not grumbling, but purring now

on my shoulder, far-off beyond a border
only the dream can cross,

so I'd wheel toward home,
and suddenly in the dirty half-light flooding the neighborhood,

the block wouldn't look half so ratty.
And somewhere behind us a radio would blare

a happy song, and on the curb across the street,
the neighborhood grouch in his bathrobe would nod

and wave his morning news. Even those eggbeaters rattling
into rush hour would almost seem benevolent.

So I'd slow a little, watchful of the cracked sidewalk,
the blind drives, dragging out the moment

as the sun threw an aura over chimneys
and buckled rooftops, banked its fireworks

off upstairs windows, and I'd slow a little more, hugging
the blanket close, terrified of this new joy

on my shoulder,
delighted that the neighborhood, like me, was waking up.

I

WRESTLING ANGELS

for J. and Diana Stege

With crowbars and drag chains
we walk tonight through a valley of tombs
where the only sounds are frogs in the reeds
and the river whispering at the foot of Rose Hill
that we have come to salvage from the dead.

Only the ironwork will bring us money,
ornamental sofas overlooking graves,
black-flowered fences planted in marble,
occasionally an urn or a bronze star.

But if there is time
we shatter the hourglasses,
slaughter lambs asleep on children's graves,
break the blades off stone scythes,
the marble strings on silent lyres.
Only the angels are here to stop us, and they have grown
too weak to wrestle.
We break their arms and leave them wingless,
leaning over graves like old men lamenting their age.

SHOOTING RATS AT THE BIBB COUNTY DUMP

Loaded on beer and whiskey, we ride
to the dump in carloads
to turn our headlights across the wasted field,
freeze the startled eyes of rats against mounds of rubbish.

Shot in the head, they jump only once, lie still
like dead beer cans.
Shot in the gut or rump, they writhe and try to burrow
into garbage, hide in old truck tires,
rusty oil drums, cardboard boxes scattered across the mounds,
or else drag themselves on forelegs across our beams of light
toward the darkness at the edge of the dump.

It's the light they believe kills.
We drink and load again, let them crawl
for all they're worth into the darkness we're headed for.

BELOW FREEZING ON PINELOG MOUNTAIN

Crouched in the rusted cab of a junked pulpwood truck,
we take shelter from freezing rain,
count bullet holes shot in the hood by hunters.

Our burden is keeping dry
while dogs follow the game into darker woods,
white breath rising from their yelps like spirits
in that song land *where the soul never dies.*
But when you pass me the bottle,
cough for the whiskey burning
cold in your throat, that same breath fogs the windshield,
rises like gray smoke through rust holes in the roof.

A TRUCKER DRIVES THROUGH HIS LOST YOUTH

Years ago he drove a different route.
Hauling in a stripped-out Ford
the white hill whiskey nightclubs paid good money for,
he ran backroads from Ballground to Atlanta
with the cunning of a fox,
hung on each county's dirt curves like a banking hawk.

He remembers best how driving with no headlights
the black Ford felt for the road like a bat
and how his own eyes, groping at first for moonlight,
learned to cut through darkness like an owl's.
Sometimes he drove those black roads on instinct alone.

As the shadow of a bridge falls across his face,
his rear-view says he is not the same man.
Still tonight when there is no traffic, no patrol,
no streetlight to cast shadows or light the center line,
he will search again for the spirit
behind the eyes in his rear-view mirror.
Tonight in open country in heavenly darkness
the interstate to Atlanta will crumble into gravel and sand,
median and shoulder will fall into pine forest,
and his foot will floor the stripped-out Ford
till eighteen wheels roll, roll, roll
him backwards as far as his mind will haul.

STUMPTOWN ATTENDS THE PICTURE SHOW

on the first attempt at desegregation in Canton, Georgia

Word has come and Martha the ticket girl
stands behind the candy counter
eating popcorn and smoking Salems.
Beside her the projectionist,
having canned Vivien Leigh
and come downstairs to watch the real show,
leans folding chairs against the theater doors,
guards his glass counter
like saloon keepers in his Westerns
guard the mirrors hung above their bars.

Outside, good old boys line the sidewalk,
string chain between parking meters
in front of the Canton Theater,
dig in like Rebs in a Kennesaw trench.
From the street, policemen and sheriff's deputies
address their threats to proper names,
try to maintain any stability.
Someone has already radioed the State Boys.

Through the glass door Martha watches
the moon slide over Jones Mercantile.
In front of Landers' Drugstore
a streetlight flickers like a magic lantern,
but Martha cannot follow the plot,
neither can the projectionist.
One thing is certain:
elements from different worlds are converging,
spinning toward confrontation,
and the State Boys are winding down some county road,
moving in a cloud of dust toward the theater marquee.

JAMMING WITH THE BAND AT THE VFW

I played old Country and Western
then sat alone at a table near the bandstand,
smug in the purple light
that seemed like a bruised sun
going down over Roswell, Georgia.

A short bald man in a black string tie
and a woman with a red beehive
waltzed across the floor
like something out of Lawrence Welk,
his hips moving like a metronome in baggy pants,
her following like a mirror image.

For a long time I watched and drank beer,
listened to the tear-jerking music,
thought of all my written words,
all the English classes, the workshops,
the MA stored safely under my cowboy hat,
the arty sophisticates
who attend readings in Atlanta

and weighed against them
not one bald man waltzing a woman through another Blitz,
but all men turning gray who dream of having died
at Anzio, Midway, Guadalcanal.

Then rising from my chair
I drank the last of the Pabst
and moved through the bruised light of the bandstand
onto the purple dance floor, toward the tables
across the room, toward the table beside the bar,
and there the woman with platinum hair
and rhinestone earrings, moving suddenly toward me.

WRITING ON NAPKINS AT THE SUNSHINE CLUB

Macon, Georgia, 1970

The Rock-O-La plays Country and Western
three for a quarter and nothing recorded since 1950.
A man with a heart
tattoo had a five dollar thing for Hank and Roy,
over and over the same tunes
till someone at the bar asked to hear a woman's voice.

All night long I've been sitting in this booth
watching beehives and tight skirts,
gold earrings glowing and fading in the turning light
of a Pabst Blue Ribbon sign,
beer guts going purple and yellow and orange
around the Big Red Man pinball machine.

All night a platinum blonde has brought beer
to the table,
asked if I'm writing love letters on the folded napkins,
and I've been unable to answer her
or find any true words to set down on the wrinkled paper.
What needs to be written is caught already
in Hank's lonesome wail,
the tattooed arm of the man who's all quarters,
the hollow ring and click of the tilted Red Man,
even the low belch of the brunette behind the flippers.

CALLING ACROSS WATER AT LION COUNTRY SAFARI

Across Reptile Pond a herd of zebra graze in open green
captivity, black-striped necks bent to bales of hay
dropped by natives from truck beds.
An ostrich trots into the herd
and a few colts break toward a tree by the green canal
where a giraffe neck thin as straw
needles the leaves of lower branches.

On Ape Island a gibbon moves like a gray blur
through the limbs of a leafless tree.
Below him two chimps leaning on their knuckles
watch our cars roll by in procession
something like a line of elephants in a circus.
In the back seat our Safari guide
speaks through the taped drumbeats of a darker continent,
warns against leaving cars or throwing food.

But a silverback gorilla in the mouth of a cave
sees my lens spark against the sunlight.
His hairy arm stretching slowly toward the car
curls back to his chest.
My shutter catches his eye,
the long talking arm circling in and out, calling me
across water, the only thing he believes is really between us.

REST AT THE MERCY HOUSE

Because nature doesn't specialize
in mercy, this House of Refuge was raised behind the dunes
on Gilbert's Bar,
provisioned with fuel and blankets, cereals
and dried meat, for the survivors of ships wrecked
on offshore reefs. And in its time
adequate to its vision.

Now with others
we parade behind the hatchery and marvel
how the newborn turtles cobble the bottom of their tank,
wander past aquariums of native fish,
tap our fingers against the glass, little codes
we want them to know us by, then tread
the boardwalk down to the beach
where survivors in another time waded
toward shore with whatever they could salvage,
mostly themselves.
                    No more shipwrecks
off this coast, only a few survivors of wrecked
or uncharted lives, a few tourists
looking for a place to beach. Across the dunes
the sea oats wash back and forth in a gold froth.
Gulls and black skimmers, pelicans and terns,
take sanctuary in the weathered hollows of the sea wall.
Here nothing is molested, all blest.
For travelers like us, a tour of the house, a vision,
a momentary rest.

A HOME BUYER WATCHES THE MOON

The whole neighborhood is quiet.
The architect who lives across the street
is now the architect of dreams, his cedar split-level
still as a crypt on the landscaped hill.
In the brick ranch house
the city planner turns another spadeful of dirt,
a groundbreaking for his own monument. And I,
who can no longer afford to live
in my two-story, have come out into the street
to stare past the mailboxes at an abrupt dead end.

Quietly now the bats jerk
in and out of the streetlight, their shadows
zipping across the grass like black snakes.
And the moon lies balanced on the roof of my house
like a new gold coin, or the simple face
of an angel in a Colonial cemetery.

SIGN FOR MY FATHER, WHO STRESSED THE BUNT

On the rough diamond,
the hand-cut field below the dog lot and barn,
we rehearsed the strict technique
of bunting. I watched from the infield,
the mound, the backstop
as your left hand climbed the bat, your legs
and shoulders squared toward the pitcher.
You could drop it like a seed
down either base line. I admired your style,
but not enough to take my eyes off the bank
that served as our center-field fence.

Years passed, three leagues of organized ball,
no few lives. I could homer
into the garden beyond the bank,
into the left-field lot of Carmichael Motors,
and you still stressed the same technique,
the crouch and spring, the lead arm absorbing
just enough impact. That whole tiresome pitch
about basics never changing,
and I never learned what you were laying down.

Like a hand brushed across the bill of a cap,
let this be the sign
I'm getting a grip on the sacrifice.

UNDER THE BOATHOUSE

Out of my clothes, I ran past the boathouse
to the edge of the dock
and stood before the naked silence of the lake,
on the drive behind me, my wife
rattling keys, calling for help with the grill,
the groceries wedged into the trunk.
Near the tail end of her voice, I sprang
from the homemade board, bent body
like a hinge, and speared the surface,
cut through water I would not open my eyes in,
to hear the junked depth pop in both ears
as my right hand dug into silt and mud,
my left hand clawed around a pain.
In a fog of rust I opened my eyes to see
what had me, and couldn't but knew
the fire in my hand and the weight of the thing
holding me under, knew the shock of all
things caught by the unknown
as I kicked off the bottom like a frog,
my limbs doing fearfully strange strokes,
lungs collapsed in a confusion of bubbles,
all air rising back to its element.
I flailed after it, rose toward the bubbles
breaking on light, then felt down my arm
a tug running from a taut line.
Halfway between the bottom of the lake
and the bottom of the sky, I hung like a buoy
on a short rope, an effigy
flown in an underwater parade,
and imagined myself hanging there forever,
a curiosity among fishes, a bait hanging up
instead of down. In the lung-ache,
in the loud pulsing of temples, what gave first

was something in my head, a burst
of colors like the blind see, and I saw
against the surface a shadow like an angel
quivering in a dead-man's float,
then a shower of plastic knives and forks
spilling past me in the lightened water, a can
of barbequed beans, a bottle of A.1., napkins
drifting down like white leaves,
heavenly litter from the world I struggled toward.
What gave then was something on the other end,
and my hand rose on its own and touched my face.
Into the splintered light under the boathouse,
the loved, suffocating air hovering over the lake,
the cry of my wife leaning dangerously
over the dock, empty grocery bags at her feet,
I bobbed with a hook through the palm of my hand.

THE COPPERHEAD

A dwarfed limb
or a fist-thick vine, he lay stretched
across a dead oak fallen into the water.
I saw him when I cast my lure
toward a cluster of stumps near the half-buried trunk,
then pulled the boat to the edge of the limbs.
One ripple ran up his back like the tail
of a wake,
and he lay still again, dark and patterned,
large on years of frogs and rats.

I worked the lure around the brush,
oak and poplar stumps rising out of the water
like the ruins of an old pier,
and watched his spade head shift on the dry bark.
But no bass struck
so I laid the rod across the floor of the boat,
sat for a long time watching the shadows
make him a part of the tree,
and wanted more than once to drift into the shaded water,
pull myself down a fallen branch toward the trunk
where he lay quiet and dangerous and unafraid,
all spine and nerve.

IN A JON BOAT DURING A FLORIDA DAWN

Sunlight displaces stars
and on the Wakulla
long cypress shadows streak water burning
light and clear. If you look around you,
as you must, you see the bank dividing itself
into lights and darks, black waterbugs
stirring around algae beds, watermarks circling
gray trunks of cypress and oak,
a cypress knee fading under a darker moccasin,
silver tips of river grass breaking
through lighted water, silver backs of mullet
streaking waves of river grass.
For now, there are no real colors, only tones
promising change, a sense
of something developing, and no matter
how many times you have been here,
in this boat or another,
you feel an old surprise surfacing
in and around you. If you could,
you would cut the outboard
and stop it all right here at the gray height
of that anticipation. You would hide yourself
in this moment, cling to an oak branch
or a river snag
and stop even the slightest drift of the current.
In fresh sunlight distinguishing loggerhead
from stump, moss from stone,
you would give yourself completely
to the holding,
like the lizard clinging to the reed cover
or the red tick anchored in the pit of your knee.

IN A U-HAUL NORTH OF DAMASCUS

1

Lord, what are the sins
I have tried to leave behind me? The bad checks,
the workless days, the Scotch bottles thrown across the fence
and into the woods, the cruelty of silence,
the cruelty of lies, the jealousy,
the indifference?

What are these on the scale of sin
or failure
that they should follow me through the streets of Columbus,
the moon-streaked fields between Benevolence
and Cuthbert where dwarfed cotton sparkles like pearls
on the shoulders of the road? What are these
that they should find me half-lost,
sick and sleepless
behind the wheel of this U-Haul truck parked in a field on Georgia 45
a few miles north of Damascus,
some makeshift rest stop for eighteen wheelers
where the long white arms of oaks slap across trailers
and headlights glare all night through a wall of pines?

2

What was I thinking, Lord?
That for once I'd be in the driver's seat, a firm grip
on direction?

So the jon boat muscled up the ramp,
the Johnson outboard, the bent frame of the wrecked Harley
chained for so long to the back fence,

the scarred desk, the bookcases and books,
the mattress and box springs,
a broken turntable, a Pioneer amp, a pair
of three-way speakers, everything mine
I intended to keep. Everything else abandon.

But on the road from one state
to another, what is left behind nags back through the distance,
a last word rising to a scream, a salad bowl
shattering against a kitchen cabinet, china barbs
spiking my heel, blood trailed across the cream linoleum
like the bedsheet that morning long ago
just before I watched the future miscarried.

Jesus, could the irony be
that suffering forms a stronger bond than love?

3

Now the sun
streaks the windshield with yellow and orange, heavy beads
of light drawing highways in the dew-cover.
I roll down the window and breathe the pine-air,
the after-scent of rain, and the far-off smell
of asphalt and diesel fumes.

But mostly pine and rain
as though the world really could be clean again.

Somewhere behind me,
miles behind me on a two-lane that streaks across
west Georgia, light is falling
through the windows of my half-empty house.
Lord, why am I thinking about this? And why should I care
so long after everything has fallen

to pain that the woman sleeping there should be sleeping alone?
Could I be just just another sinner who needs to be blinded
before he can see? Lord, is it possible to fall
toward grace? Could I be moved
to believe in new beginnings? Could I be moved?

IN THE ICE PASTURE

Something cried in the field and I took the binoculars
into the yard, the zeroing wind,
saw in what starlight the glasses gathered
the gray barn, the empty pasture haunted
with trees, nothing.
And then in patches the deep prints
tracking the hill, the snow trail floating
over the broken fence
where the horse walked fifty yards onto the pond
to fall neck-deep through the ice.

What was he trying to become out there,
thrashing to get a hoof up
like an odd beast cracking his shell?

I ran to the basement for an ax
and out the basement door, outrunning my breath
to the edge of the bank,
where he calmed to watch me tap with the handle,
creep three-legged onto the pond,
as though he wanted me to witness the beauty
of his change—only a quiver of the head
as he waited,
half a white statue in a fountain of ice.

Sleet, like static, crackled the pond
as I eased him back from the blade of the ax.
Then behind me a noise like the snapping of bones
and my feet stood on nothing as I grabbed
for his mane, sank chest-deep
in the shock of the cold,
both of us sinking, hooves
pounding legs, kicking me under.

How long did I hang there, numb,
bodiless, before the body of the horse rose under me
and what we were lunged hard, broke
to the air, to the wind turning us scaly
with water?

The sleet blistered the pond, the ice groaned.
Then the first kick. And the hacking, the snorting,
till the roar we made broke up the dark
in the throats of dogs, the cattle bedded
in the field, broke by inches the black shell
of water, till the night
cracked like an egg shattered in the storm
of two beasts becoming one,
or one beast being born.

HOMAGE TO LESTER FLATT

Troublesome waters I'm fearing no more

Five seasons without traveling to a festival, without walking
into a field and hearing that voice.

And now after a long spell of rain, I step off my porch
and walk toward the river,
remembering the last time I saw Lester Flatt,
how thin he looked and sick
as he sat back in a lawn chair under the sagging pines
of Lavonia, Georgia,
and scribbled his name on the jackets of records.

How do the roots chord, Lester?
And the click beetle and the cricket, the cicada, the toad,
what harmonies do they sing in the high grass?

All of those voices
want me to praise your remarkable voice—

Tonight little sparks are winking in the fields, and the dead
are combing the edge of the forest, their arms
full of campfires.
Tonight the dead are building a stage under a funeral tent
and blowing the dust off banjos.
Tonight, for you, the dead are shaking the worms
from their ears.

Lester, singing whatever we want to about the dead
is the easiest thing in the world.
Believing it the hardest.
So this is where I stop, in this wet grass.
This is the river we're all troubled by, where the storm wash
rattling the bank echoes the tenor of our lives.

UNDER THE VULTURE-TREE

We have all seen them circling pastures,
have looked up from the mouth of a barn, a pine clearing,
the fences of our own backyards, and have stood
amazed by the one slow wing beat, the endless dihedral drift.
But I had never seen so many so close, hundreds,
every limb of the dead oak feathered black,

and I cut the engine, let the river grab the jon boat
and pull it toward the tree.
The black leaves shined, the pink fruit blossomed
red, ugly as a human heart.
Then, as I passed under their dream, I saw for the first time
its soft countenance, the raw fleshy jowls
wrinkled and generous, like the faces of the very old
who have grown to empathize with everything.

And I drifted away from them, slow, on the pull of the river,
reluctant, looking back at their roost,
calling them what I'd never called them, what they are,
those dwarfed transfiguring angels,
who flock to the side of the poisoned fox, the mud turtle
crushed on the shoulder of the road,
who pray over the leaf-graves of the anonymous lost,
with mercy enough to consume us all and give us wings.

NAVAL PHOTOGRAPH: 25 OCTOBER 1942: WHAT THE HAND MAY BE SAYING

Reports of a Japanese surface presence have brought them speeding
into Savo Sound,
false reports that won't be true for days.

So now at evening the fleet drops anchor, the crews relax,
the heat drifts west toward the war in Africa.

On the deck of the tender *Tangier*
a sailor focuses a camera on a foreground of water,
the cruiser *Atlanta,* and far back against the jungles of Savo
the hulks of Task Group 66.4.

A few on the cruiser notice him, but you can't tell
from their faces, too many shadows, too long a stretch
of grainy water. Still,
figures can be seen loafing on the bow, leaning
from the bridge, the machine gun platforms, even a sailor
clowning on a gun turret, barrel straight up between his legs.

And behind the shadow draped like armor across that stern,
my father is standing with the gunners
under turret number six, a shadow
in a wide cluster of shadows waving toward the *Tangier.*

Knowing their future, I imagine
some pulse in the nerves, primitive as radar, throbbing,
and exactly what the hand is saying, even he doesn't know.
He is only standing where the living and the dead
lean against the rail,
unsure who is who, and wave across the sound
toward the camera, toward us, for all of the reasons anyone waves.

THE ANNIVERSARY

This is the night I come to my room,
a bottle of brandy, or whiskey, a glass,
and close the door on the rest of the house,
pull the shades, switch off the lights,
imagine a darkness just as it may have been.
I pull my chair to the middle of the room,
fall to it like a man with a mission,
and do not turn on the radio, the stereo,
as I might do on any other night,
but listen to the pines brush the house
with a sound like the bow of a ship
rising and falling through water.
Then I drink for the shakes and I get them
when I see again jarring the darkness
the terrible rising sun, the searchlight
of the *Hiei* stabbing across the sound,
and jolt in my chair as the turret slues,
guns already deafening the long light blind.
Look, there he is at the door of the turret
and then, God, the blast of the shell
kicks him right back out! Then, God . . .
what? For this is the night my father,
forehead shattered, side pierced, was thrown
for dead from the deck of the *Atlanta,*
toward a place that was not Guadalcanal
or Florida Island, drifted like a man dead
to the world ending around him, and was dead
to the arms of the sailors in the lifeboat,
dead as any drunk in any armchair
who trembles at the horror of his thoughts
and learns, as he learns every year
that the power in the blood to terrify
is sometimes the power of love. So moves

one knee trembling toward his desk,
stands on shaky legs and puts down his glass,
leans on the desk and opens the drawer,
feels for the small pearl-handled knife,
the sharpest blade of Japanese steel,
This is your blood in remembrance of you,
who died one night at sea and lived,
brings it to his face, brings it to his eye,
touches with the nervous point
the flesh of his forehead, an old scar.

THE DESK

Under the fire escape, crouched, one knee in cinders,
I pulled the ball-peen hammer from my belt,
cracked a square of window pane,
the gummed latch, and swung the window,
crawled through that stone hole into the boiler room
of Canton Elementary School, once Canton High,
where my father served three extra years
as star halfback and sprinter.
                              Behind a flashlight's
cane of light, I climbed a staircase almost a ladder
and found a door. On the second nudge of my shoulder,
it broke into a hallway dark as history,
at whose end lay the classroom I had studied
over and over in the deep obsession of memory.

I swept that room with my light—an empty blackboard,
a metal table, a half-globe lying on the floor
like a punctured basketball—then followed
that beam across the rows of desks,
the various catalogs of lovers, the lists
of all those who would and would not do what,
until it stopped on the corner desk of the back row,
and I saw again, after many years the name
of my father, my name, carved deep into the oak top.

To gauge the depth I ran my finger across that scar,
and wondered at the dreams he must have lived
as his eyes ran back and forth
from the cinder yard below the window
to the empty practice field
to the blade of his pocket knife etching carefully
the long, angular lines of his name,
the dreams he must have laid out one behind another

like yard lines, in the dull, pre-practice afternoons
of geography and civics, before he ever dreamed
of Savo Sound or Guadalcanal.
                                        In honor of dreams
I sank to my knees on the smooth, oiled floor,
and stood my flashlight on its end.
Half the yellow circle lit the underedge of the desk,
the other threw a half-moon on the ceiling,
and in that split light I tapped the hammer
easy up the overhang of the desk top. Nothing gave
but the walls' sharp echo, so I swung again,
and again harder, and harder still in half anger
rising to anger at the stubborn joint, losing all fear
of my first crime against the city, the county,
the state, whatever government claimed dominion,
until I had hammered up in the ringing dark
a salvo of crossfire, and on a frantic recoil glanced
the flashlight, the classroom spinning black
as a coma.

            I've often pictured the face of the teacher
whose student first pointed to that topless desk,
the shock of the slow hand rising from the back row,
their eyes meeting over the question of absence.
I've wondered too if some low authority of the system
discovered that shattered window,
and finding no typewriters, no business machines,
no audiovisual gear missing, failed to account for it,
so let it pass as minor vandalism.
                                        I've heard nothing.
And rarely do I fret when I see that oak scar leaning
against my basement wall, though I wonder what it means
to own my father's name.

ARMORED HEARTS

I'd been awakened before by hammers cracking across the pond,
but who'd be building at dawn? On a Sunday?

And I remembered the ducks, a loggerhead
must have eaten another duck. So I rolled into my jeans
and walked out onto the porch. Then the crack again,
and I saw through the fog dusting the banks and the pond
a man on the far bank, my neighbor
in the branches of a tree, his pistol
pecking at the water, and just the right angle
to catch my house with a ricochet.

Whatever new threat I shouted
must have worked. That afternoon he took to traps,
baiting his hooks with livers and fish heads,
floating them under milk jugs. All evening
I watched from my porch as he labored in his boat, knotting
his lines, tying his bait, easing out the jugs
like a rope of pearls,
and learned how much he cared for those ducks—

and how he must have hated what killed them, the snappers
with their ugly armored hearts, who wallow
like turnips in the muck of the bottom, clinging
to their stony solitude,
who refuse to sun, hiding like lost
fears, rising when they're least expected
into a panic of wings. This is what I thought about
as I rowed in the dark from one jug to the next, stripping
the bait from his hooks.

IN A KITCHEN, LATE

If you stumble in the night out of your room of sleep
and step barefoot into the hall,
if you cross the dining room of close shadows, going
by touch along the edge of the table, the back
of a chair, the sideboard,
and stand in the doorway to the rich dark
of the kitchen, you can hear
over your held breath
a small stirring around the dog bowls.
And if you make yourself a part of the room, ease
along the counter to the fridge, pour its cold light
gently on the floor,
there they are—glossy carapace and brown wings,
always chasing the edge of the shadow.

It's good to sit in the dark in the rocker by the window,
your feet on the cool linoleum, to snack
on chicken and gaze across the deck
at the lake falling away from your fence, the woods
you'd love to be a part of. A pure loneliness,
watching needles buff the window with a darkness
you feel somehow you miss.

And if you wait long enough, without rocking,
making yourself no presence in the room,
they'll bring back
in perfect innocence through the veins of the house
their own small portion
of the night—out of the baseboards
and heater vents, faithful
as your ugliest desire, a stir
like a breath in the hairs of your leg.

LAST NICKEL RANCH: PLAINS, MONTANA

In the living room of the trailer, the father of the woman
I love calls the family into a huddle.
Dinner is over, the charcoal is ash on the grill.
Through the kitchen window, I watch the rain drifting
like a ghost across the Cabinet Mountains.
We're leaving now,
and it's time for prayer.

The family circles to a hug and calls me in,
and for a moment, silence. Wind shakes
the tin sheets roofing the deck, the lambs
bleat from the hill behind us.
I think of prayer
and the humility necessary for prayer.

Then a small squall of feathers from the guinea coop,
and in the corral
the burros scuffle against the water trough.
Hands join hands, and I catch the eagle's shadow

slicing down the ridge, one dark
blade of muscle
beautiful for its singularity.

I know what I've valued.
Last night I heard a coyote howling off the ridge
and went to the window.
In the darkness behind the glass
I saw myself, and behind my eyes the stars flew
into the pines.

HARD EASTER, NORTHWEST MONTANA

Shadows from the spruce woods slouch down the hill,
the windmill's crippled shadow
pierces the house, a blue fog spirits
the trees and the full moon
floods the empty corral. Near the dark edge
of a scream, I hunch toward the Tensor,
working at the window
on taxes. The bleak numbers blur.

On the hillside the burro watches the moon.
How saintly she seemed this morning, half-blind
and motherly, bearing
her little cross,
leading the sheep to pasture,
and saintly now, frozen against the hill
by whatever weaves
the treeline, heard or felt.

A loose tarp flaps across the firewood
as wind creaks the deck,
and steadily the ridge shadows turn
under the moon,
the windmill's shadow follows the barn.
Such a picture of peace—
burro and sheep
grazing knapweed in the late snow.

Already they've forgotten the lamb's torn lung,
the purple knot of bowels
on stained rock,
while in the mountains beyond downed fences,
muscles stretch and shudder, sharp eyes
open underground.

A DAUGHTER'S FEVER

Dark ivy draws a wave across the yard,
even the shadows
are streaked with rain. Light drizzles the oak leaves
and I rock behind this screen,
listening to squirrels, the bickering of jays.
The five a.m. garbage truck
doesn't wake you
as it scrapes the curb from can to can.
Three hours of crying lit the windows next door,
but now you lie as quiet
as the rain. After the dozen books,
the trail we frayed from piano
to puppets, to the cardboard frog
on his pond of cut wool,
I lean to your blanket
and hold my breath.

Rachel, about the little girl
who started home late
across the darkening woods . . .
Someday I'll give you the words I used all night
to guide her home. So many ways
to enter the forest and never return.
But happily that's another ending.

Under a basket of cornflowers
hung from the mantel,
she sleeps now in her cottage near the town.
Her father watches
new light clothe the trees.
In his orchard
the crows out-cackle the squirrels.

He holds his breath to hear
her breathe, around his finger
small fingers curl.

MY PERFECT NIGHT

First a tumble of clouds, muscular and black, full of noise,
then a star in a rift, remote
as a promise you intended to make. A moon, of course,
or half a moon battering those clouds with metallic light.
In my perfect night I hang this
over a clearing, a pasture, say, circled by woods.
Cows in their gentle bodies
sleep near the woods, black leaves float
and roll on the wind.
Far in the west, but not too far,
a few bears still dream
in the shadows of the foothills, a wolf eludes
extinction to lick dew off a stone.

In my perfect night I close the door on a dark house
and walk out into myself,
into the pines full of tree frogs. Somewhere in the dark
a cottonmouth flowers,
the carcass of a deer is lathered with flies.
In my perfect night I follow a trail by the river,
and my shadow on the water
looks deep and alive.

ALLATOONA EVENING

Half a mile through a briar scrub thickening to woods,
I've lugged it like a sack of stones
and come to these shadows opening the cove.
A jon boat waits among the water lilies,
restless as wind, a paddle
in the bow, as though night were a current
to be muscled through.

On the horizon
a red glaze still treads water,
and in my silence, crickets choir the treeline.
Wave after wave, they call me to lay down
my anger. And the tree frogs
with them, barking out of the needles,
the copperhead skirting rushes,
sidling into the shallows—
lay it down, they say, on the green stones
beside this water.

A whippoorwill, an echo,
and above the drooping shoulders of the willows
delicate bats tumbling for flies—
lay it down, they say, your ambition,
which is only anger,
which sated could bring you to no better place.
Nothing is more beautiful than your emptiness,
and over the lake
these three stars soaking up twilight.

II

NIGHT STRATEGIES

I kept brushing the cloth over the pouch of her stomach,
the cherubic and slightly chafed
folds of her hips,
remembering the voice rising off my radio,
a girl in Sarajevo, sixteen,
quivering between a translator and the thuds
of local shelling.

Just after dark she'd heard shouts in the street,
trash cans knocked over, panic
and the rumble of trucks,
and was crossing the room to blow out a lamp
when a soldier kicked in the door.

That dry wind in her throat,
what did it whisper about the authority of grief?

And when he pulled out of her,
when he buckled and holstered his pistol,
he went to the window and called in two comrades.
They left her naked on a bloody cot.
She wept, she said, but not inconsolably
like her mother, who clawed all night at the tiles
of their mosque.

I lathered the cloth with our wafer of soap
and dabbed at my daughter's stomach and thighs,
knowing the only answer I have
is this nervous
exaggeration of tenderness,
and that every ministry of my hand, clumsy
and apologetic, asks her
to practice such a radical faith.

COUNTRY STORE AND MOMENT OF GRACE

for Richard Bausch, Joe Hendricks & Tom Trimble

Oxford heels
hooked on the bottom rung, he rocks his straight chair
against his counter. Flick of his yo-yo
and he's walking the dog—wanting no trouble, pondering
in his afternoon daze the promised serenities
of the afterlife.
                    Pot-gut stove and wood sizzle,
and the raw smell of bologna and cheese, rack
of Slim Jim and jerky, Tom's Snacks,
peppermint, drift of kerosene from a paint can,
and from where he sits,
                        glassed sweetness
of stacked tobacco, Chesterfield and King Edward,
Beechnut, Red Man, Bull of the Woods.

Cold in this memory,
                    and through the barred window
the low sky flaunts the rags of winter.
A gospel quartet weaves harmonies
through the radio . . .
and the darkness seeping up from the freshly oiled floor
won't be beaten by three naked bulbs
choking on greasy cords.

꧁

Yes, and those wallowing clouds
of discontent . . .
barbershop, pool hall, beauty-parlor rumor
of discontent rising from the Ralph Bunche school . . .

Where? That shamble of brick off the Waleska Road
we pass on the way to my uncle's farm . . .
and one afternoon
when the store's jammed up around the stove,
I zip my jacket to pump a tank of gas—
rusted-out pickup, sagging
on its springs,
                    and looped around the rearview
a stiff noose
hanging like a pair of dice.

All through my childhood
I hardly heard a story unfold around that stove . . .
a curse spit onto its belly,
or a wisecrack following some trail of gossip,
but mostly grunts
                    or nothing at all
as my grandfather bagged the scribbled-out groceries.

Where were the storytellers I'd grow up
to hear about?
                    Brooding or tongue-tied,
worn-out in their walked-down boots and overalls shabby
with clay and tobacco juice,
or crippled, or sick,
                    coming straight
from the mill where they'd retched out their lungs
into smoking-booth peach cans,
                                        weak
and lint-crowned, wanting to get home.

In middle age,
in those first leaf-turns before the smudging into winter
when the bird feeders are abandoned

to squirrels and frost
and everything alive is sacking it up
                                or packing
it in for the season,
the memory becomes portentous,
                                like some newfound gospel
promising, finally, the whole fantastic story
and unscrolling into fragments.

～

Brass glow of charcoal
and stench of beefsteak rising into the low clouds,

all over the suburb burnt offerings going up
under the drizzle of leaves . . .

Rachel rakes a few into a pile the wind disperses,
and again I'm drawing parallels
to the memory . . .
                        gusts behind the eyelids,
mulch of the cosmic swirl . . .

～

Eleven or twelve, I bop into the store . . .

blue smoke around the woodstove
                                where a few men lean
against the ice-cream box—the man with a hook
who left his hand in Italy,
the logger who walks on the side of his foot,
another I don't know
scraping his thumbnail with the blade of a barlow—
jeans and jackets, a cap with earflaps,
scrub beards icing into sideburns.

I squeeze past the bread counter
and jerk a few balloons from a glass jar, water bombs
for the Boy Scouts.

The clubfoot grins, shaking peanuts
into his Coke bottle.

My grandfather, saying nothing, rings the cash register,
and the blue Prince Albert drifts
across the store.
          Blood rush and the white haze
of laughter . . .

Whose laughter? And who am I here
pushing through the screen and into the air?

～

Blam! and shoulder-kick
and the barbed stink of gunpowder blowing across the field,
one or two targets
          rattle on their wires
and behind them a trembling of needles and leaves
dangling over that outfield fence . . .

Turkey shoot sponsored by the Canton Little League,
and me running targets
across a pasture
          my father has turned into a diamond . . .

Smudge pots glowing
through rust, folding table of shotguns, cherished
blued steel cradled in the plush
of unzipped cases,
and a lost face at the judge's table
          shuffles a stack

of riddled targets, gauging in a huddle of men
the two pellet holes
closest to the center of the cross.

Compass legs rise off a target,
my grandfather's pellet
                    a chicken whisker off.

～

Those little self-judgments, needle jabs of regret . . .
easy enough to stomach
with a shake of the head, a sour grin,
then the grim walk home, alone,
                              pockets empty, sky empty . . .

and late into the night
those prickly fingers of moonlight
pointing from the bedroom wall, those sweaty sheets,
that black noose of fuchsia
                    dangling from the planter.

～

Whenever I think I know about grief,
I imagine an only son lost
in the Pacific,
                    an ear to the Philco for sketchy news . . .
Coral Sea, Midway, Guadalcanal . . .
and picture my grandmother collapsing one morning
by the mailbox,
crushed letter like a rock in her hand.

Fifteen months she thought him dead
                              and fell every evening
at the altar of Oakdale

until a woman in the church dreamed him wounded
but faceup,
                    alive in burning water . . .

Tears and worn-out prayer bones
and everything else is gravy—
                                King James Bible,
ragged paperback *Gone With the Wind,*
green stamps, soda caps,
a few mail orders collecting around Christmas . . .
pans of Dr. Pepper
                        heating on the stove . . .
rags for quilts, a box of buttons,
thimbles and needles,

and unraveling off-key in the kitchen
the scratchy thread of one old song,
                            when the shadows
of this life have grown . . .

Yes, late into the night while the gray needles
slap the window
and again at sunrise, and again on the last waves of light
sifting through these shedding maples . . .

like the spring catalog of Montgomery Ward, waterlogged
and fat as a Masonic Bible,
                            sprawling three days
in their drive, drying its leaves in the sun.

I've robbed it from the mailbox
straight to the yard swing
to savor it most of the afternoon—
                            the spinners and lures,

those willowy rods that thrashed the riffles
of northern rivers . . .

So when I leave it open
in the swing to soak up an hour of evening rain,
I'm not stunned
to find it like something hurt
                                        wrapped in towels
on the kitchen porch,
nor stunned now to glimpse again her face
that only time I saw her weep.

~

Sputter of choked engine, cough
and snarl,
              and a spume of dusty smoke wallows the back fence.
Our neighbor, the broker, revving his leaf blower . . .
like a bird from prison bars has flown,
and the oily cloud sifts through the trees . . .
so be it. Yes, so be it. Amen to the tidy suburban driveway,
to all souls sweeping up loose scraps.

Jesus of Oakdale,
                    of Philadelphia and Macedonia,
Savior of the lost souls of Shiloh,
who stills the heart's waters at the altar of Soul Harbor,
raise your staff out of those stained windows
and shepherd these sheep
                              across the hills of remorse.

~

A hundred yards south of my grandfather's grocery—
ours is the scrawny house of green shingles, rusted screens
on the side porch,
rock arch around the door.

Television in the living room, Arthur Godfrey
or Ed Sullivan, and a juggler spins plates on tall sticks
as my father and I watch from the couch . . .
Sweet smell of corn
and barbecued chicken,

                  which means it's Sunday . . .

Horns blare from the highway, south from the Trading Post,
loud and louder,
then right outside our door
                      a legion of noise.
I jump toward the window
and get jerked back,
              my father's fist on my belt, holding,
his head shaking, a look on his face.

My mother walks in from the kitchen, dishrag wringing
a water glass. Her eyebrows wrinkle . . .

three or four minutes before the Empire passes.

⁓

Lipscomb, Lusk, Dilworth, Pope,
the names wash in
like familiar smells—pine straw, dog lot, cow manure,
leather tack and the wet hides of horses—
tough as their ax handles, blunt
as the pistol butts hanging from their pockets,
though not the tall man in his eternal bibs
frayed at every corner and crease,
who on Saturdays leaned over the ice-cream box
like a mourner
              over a casket,
and brought out for the small girl in coat-rags
near the grill of the stove
                  one frostbitten hunky.

Depression-era photo, sharp bone, tow hair,
sagging eyes . . .
                        and though she hears nothing,
and speaks it back like a Holiness tongue,
all rough talk has ceased,
                                        the air
she moves through like an aisle of grace.

The man with one arm
                                puts a Hershey's in her palm,
another fills her pocket with peanuts.
Smoke and shadows . . .
                                but nothing
in those shadows as luminous as her face.

꧁

Close it down, Dilworth says . . .

Swish of a blade on a slick whetstone, and out the window
a yellow frenzy of snow . . .

Close it down, he says,
                        fore I let Lyndon Johnson run it.

Dilworth, the roughest and loudest,
though none are boasters or idle talkers.

So nods Lipscomb, so nods Lusk.

And what more frightening
                                than a roomful of quiet men?

꧁

A Christmas story often told.
Canton, Georgia: black section, Stumptown,

and who has seen snow only twice in her life,
and that so long ago
                    she recalls it as sugar, flour, salt,
sits in her kitchen all morning
and through the clear windowpane
watches a sky staining gray
                    over a bristled ridge of pine.

He's late today,
                    which means the woods behind the school
will be one pine less thick,
which means the Singer will need to be rolled
into the bedroom, the rocker drawn
to the side
              of the fireplace,
which means the balls of cloth and glass
can come out of their boxes
                              in the hall closet . . .
mistletoe and pine boughs,
candles lined on the window sills . . .

And as the sky over the ridge thickens like night,
she thinks of stars,
                    cinnamon stars
sprinkled over icy borders of cake, stars of red tinsel
hanging from the mantel,
                          the heavy brass star shining
like gold behind the white candle,
the evening star rising behind those clouds
like a bright eye
burning, unseen, all night.

Then who has seen snow only twice in her life,
who thinks she loves
                    every kind of star, sees climbing
the road beside her house
the dull yellow star on the door of a Chevy

and feels down her nerves
                              the ice
of her whole head frosting white, a shiver
against terrible weather.

⁓

True story. Small-town courthouse, movie-set live oaks
sagging over a scruffy lawn, cigar butts
and acorn-fall,
                    marble steps up to the marble portico,
and climbing them one out-of-town lawyer,
young and wiry, dapper in suit, bow tie, suspenders,
not yet a headliner,
                    not yet the winner of big cases.
A civil suit
in the county seat of corruption . . .
already he knows the defendant's attorney
is the judge's brother. Still, the truth and the law.

First question from the judge,
"Mr. Cook, have you and your client made an honest attempt
to settle this case?"
                    Bobby Lee stands up
and strokes his goatee,
"Why, yes sir, we made an offer of twenty thousand."
"Oh, no, Mr. Cook," the judge
shakes his head, "we couldn't possibly pay that . . . "

⁓

Dead are the corrupt
and no less dead are the less corrupt . . .
and this evening a crystal dusting of sunlight layers
the backyard with shadow and near-shadow.

Red poplar leaf and oak leaf,
                              and a few scruffy sparrows
still foraging the feeders . . .
no swaggering robins,
                    no wild canaries
with their little yellow crowns . . . *Like a bird*
from prison bars, yes. The hummingbird feeder droops
from its branch
like a Japanese lantern.

December, 1960. Weekend of rumor
and black weather blowing in from Alabama, two cars burned
on the curb in front of the Canton Theater . . .
Then that familiar crunch
of gravel as a car rolls up to his gasoline pumps.
Brooding men and veil of blue smoke
and the hot belly of the stove . . .
                              The car door shuts
but no one glances up.
Creak of the screen and the big door opening . . .

Dilworth pushes off the drink box, closes his knife,
Pope takes out his stogie and spits
on the stove.
            Sizzle
and a shifting of logs, and the high wheeze
of wood fire sucking air . . .

The woman is cotton-haired, but not quite frail,
and the black hand digging
                        into the pocket of her coat
brings out a coin purse, red and blue beaded,
like something you might buy
on a reservation.

Wood crackles
as the door cries low on cold hinges . . .

Cheated again, they see,
                              and a glassy angularity hardens
on those faces
as though each has seen history for what it is
and not for what he's imagined.

     ⁓

We go on now
building on what they were obliged to build on,
pasting into the memory
                              these little scraps of consequence
and self-acquittal,

so that it's Amen finally to what can't be changed,
to the noise of headline and newscast, feint
and bluff of history,
while the real thing
                              plays out quietly somewhere else . . .

like my grandfather rocking up
out of his chair,
                    not gauging their faces,
not glancing at me watching, stunned, from the feed room
as the woman fingered coins
and lifted from the drink box a bottle of Coca-Cola,
so that suddenly at the scripted moment
the script fell away,
                    his hand simply opening,
his head nodding slowly
as she dropped the two nickels and faded
in the drizzle, in the shiver and groan of muffler,
the crunch of tires on gravel.

And Amen now to that failure of nerve
or heart, or among those hardening glares, that victory
of nerve or heart.

Amen to its passing into memory
and Amen to its passing again out of memory . . .

Amen even to the Kmart where his grocery stood,
and the five-stall barn sagging toward the riding ring,
the hillside of pasture,
                              the kudzued chicken houses
and dog lots,
              the baseball field of my father's making
with its twelve-foot wire backstop . . .

Amen to the leaving behind of places
that might have been less lovely and often are . . .

and to the dust that walked those places
to enter by its own path
                              this fractured afterlife of memory,
and peace to the souls that abandoned that dust,
                                                  Amen.

Each evening the light forgives the darkness,
each morning the darkness forgives
the light,
          and after the final flame has fallen off
the tongue, the silence that forgives everything . . .
the loosed soul tumbling . . .

And Amen also to single-malt Scotch in the emerald dusk,
and this child with the rake-handle
taller than her head,
muscling her will against the inevitable . . .

What's left in these last moments but memory?
And what is memory
but the mirror-image of hope?

So Amen also to hope
and to these blurred receding thoughts of the evening
blowing out across the lawn furniture
                                        and barbecue grill,
leaf-drifts and scattering wind,
                            these shadows
of house and pine

and fence and maple becoming one shadow
when the shadows of this life . . .

                                yes,
lengthen into the shadow of memory,

and finally
to that shadow, Amen.

A CANOE

remembering James Dickey

Racket below us,
diesel clank
and the grate of linked steel, and on that hillside of graves
we laid down our charcoal and rice paper
to watch at yard speed and rising
a rolling curtain of freight cars blocking out the river.
Tombstones trembled near trackside—coal car,
boxcar, tanker, transport—
then behind the last wheel rattling around the crypts,
far up toward the highway, near the middle of the river,
a canoe washed under the bridge.
Red canoe. Empty.

Screech of the freight disappearing,
then a lazy ride, the canoe,
                        so we let our eyes go
with it. River untroubled, calm reflection.

On the far bank, shadowy,
three fishermen on the rocks pushed back their hats.
Long canes wagging in a glint of sunlight,
lines swept down
                  toward the hunger of carp . . .
they only slouched lower in their lawn chairs.

What deeper stirring could they hope for?
A metaphor untethered, loose
and retrievable,
               but drifting away . . .

AT THE GRAVE OF MARTHA ELLIS

Today a visitor has left a rose
at your feet
and a few of the yellow buds sprouting on the hillside,
a quarter to buy whatever it will in your stilled childhood
of 1896. Misty rain
and no sun for days, the silky tongues
of the cherry blossoms struggle at their morning prayers,
the willow and the winged elm, the mulberry
and the sweet gum
spread their budding gospel down Hawthorne Ridge.
Little Martha, these mornings of early mist
when the sun hasn't quite cleared
the carriage paths
and the breeze up the hillside oozes
honeysuckle and cherry,
the soul likes to cruise for serenity.

But you know why I've come.
Before the stone carvers turned you into marble,
you knew what it was to wander among angels,
gathering from these terraces
your Sunday bouquets while waltzers around the bandstand
strayed into the graves. Little Martha,
in middle age rebirth isn't such easy work,
though everything goes at it again
like Baptists reeling to articulate rapture,
and the morning reissues its pledge—
the mockingbird,
the crow breaking the far hush of the wind,
and in the valley above the river
white clouds of dogwood floating through the underbrush
while redwings drop like blood
through the branches.

EASTER SHOES EPISTLE

for Mark Jarman

Yesterday morning five plumbers from Sundance
dug up the pipes in our front yard—
                                    twelve feet down and roots
through a joint, a total blockage.
Now mounds of sour mud sag beside a canvas tarp, while the last rain dripping
like wax through the Bradford pears, glistens
on the boxwoods.
                    Stench and flowers, and an urgent glaze
over the neighborhood, the dogwoods already mustering an incredible witness,
and the jungles of hydrangea,
                                the Japanese cherries, the azaleas deviling
the roses, and oddly, in the street,
even an old work boot, like a shriveled potato,
rain-curled, corroded,
                        shooting its little feelers toward the curb.

Every leaf an oracle, sure,
                            and in the local phone book
not one listing under *mystagogue* . . .

ﷲ

Every spring
the world is such a tricky magician, tugging whole maple trees
out of its black silk hat, pulling thunderstorms
from its sleeve . . .

Miracle or sleight of hand
is what I fret about.
                    And the mockingbird, unconcerned, goes on worrying
the new weeds, and the cardinal,

the chipmunk homesteading the overturned wheelbarrow,
our neighbor's grouchy tabby
                              skulking about in its own eternal moment.

Only we have to travel on faith,
                              struggling not to notice the absence,
the stray shoe in the street, the fugitive foot . . .

≈

Saturday night, just after supper, aftertaste of vegetable soup
and soda crackers
washed down with chocolate milk . . .

A little blue moonlight spilling across the sink,
the pans of sudsy water,
                              the Easter petunia sagging in its grim plastic pot,
a little moonlight, I remember, slipping past the ragged pines
screening out the lights
on the radio tower . . . blue flash, blue flash . . .

Just like an old shoe, my mother said, rattling her bottle of polish,
meaning *faith*,
                    while I glanced at my loafers on the seat of a kitchen chair—
penny loafers, sans pennies, scuffed around the toes and cracking,
run-down in schoolyards, filth of pasture,
                                        polluted creek.

≈

Sometimes faith is more a stale cracker,
                                        and yet how little else
we have to share—a few words, a few dried metaphors we can lay aboard,
stocking up like Noah for that darkest flood.

Little cakes and wine,
Lawrence advised, a few cooking pots, a change of clothes.
And a good pair of shoes, I'd say,
                              a can of Kiwi, a bottle of Griffin.

≈

Or plain old saddle soap will do—
                              take my wife's boots, glassy
as a crow's eye, which I can't forget seeing
shuffling across the floor
of a cowgirl bar in Great Falls, Montana. Spanish boots, I remember,
with silver heels and toes,

Spanish boots, high-topped, waxed to a crow's eye.

≈

All morning the tiny petals of these pears
shake off in the wind, flicker and drift, as though their own small witness
is to shame us into faith . . .
                              In middle age, truly,
it's all a grueling miracle, the spirit sagging like a bag of cut grass,
or curling on itself like an old boot . . .

Everything struggling, yes,
toward severance, it's odd what the memory smuggles into the afterlife—
the squeak of my mother's hospital shoes,
or a baseball game from the fifties, my father's wing tips
kicking up a coaching box—
                              pocket charms against oblivion,

and I'd not want to forget these pear trees dusting the driveway,
the pickup, the yard,
                    or my daughter on her toes, rattling

light from low branches, I'd not forget
these petals like soggy pearls

                              clinging to her shoes.

～

When my wife was a child, she was ashamed of her shoes.

Southern California, mid-sixties . . .

                              so picture Easter with orange trees,
lemon, oleander, eucalyptus, picture small daisies
in bright window boxes along the edge
of the desert, red hue in the morning light, blue in the evening,
and now a second grader, a little girl with one dress
salvaged from a house fire

                              and worn all year to school.

Imagine shoes to match, and Easter in a child's mind.

Sure, some children have less, but put yourself in that child's mind
and picture the Cadillac pulling
into your graveled drive.

                    Surely you'd remember the crunch
of those tires, your Sunday-school teacher's teal and gold sandals
tracking the sandy grass,
and certainly for the rest of your life
the huge double doors of that Palm Springs mall revolving
into a city of light—

                    fountains of brass cherubs,
chandeliers, skylights, and that one fragile storefront of glass
where every wall sparkles with shoes.

O MANDOLIN, *O MAGNUM MYSTERIUM*

Ah, the music of the spheres, the old pawnbroker quipped, plowing his walker
down the cluttered aisle.
                              Whatever; I nod,
and cradle the beautifully scarred mandolin in my open palms—
rutted ebony fingerboard, caramel-grained face of rusty spruce,
two strings missing, bridge cracked.
                                        Torture, I thought, teaching myself
to play this thing, then pondered all the other agonies
it must have endured—
the lovers wooed and lost, the bottles dodged
in barroom discourses,
                          loneliness of widowers on their porches at night,
their hard music rising in starlight.

String pluck and fret buzz—the sound of a spooked bird.

I turned to the window to read through dust its history in scars,
my face, no doubt, the mug of a doubter.
So what, pleads the pawnbroker,
                            you'll have the mystery.

⁓

Or was that misery? The way the world guards its secrets, I mean, giving
grudgingly here, withholding there—
                            thus the mandolin,
disobedient, miscreant,
which might as well be the mystery of suffering itself.

So a little seclusion now, for thought, on the wooded bank of Triplett Pond.

High overcast shredding,
                    and a sudden freckling of sunlight

and out of the shallows under the rock dam a mallard taxis off the water,
climbs and banks,
> gone over the high wall of hardwoods.
Stray crow far off, mockingbird closer . . .
and the mandolin trilling out the indecipherable harmony of things.

I glare at the dark-grained teardrop from the luthiers of Gibson—
too short for a boat paddle,
> too heavy for Ping-Pong.
How charming, though, the polished and sunburst face,
the delicate snowflakes pearled
along its neck,
> its melancholy little sparrow-cries
fluttering over the riffled water. O, mandolin,
> *O Magnum Mysterium.*

Years ago in Macon, Georgia, I lived below a guy who played the mandolin.

Old Victorian on Coleman Hill, run-down
and broken into apartments,
> bad plumbing, suicidal staircase.
Late at night
> and early in the morning, as though they were expecting
a guest, the notes of his mandolin crept down the stairs
to linger on the landing.

Sometimes I'd open my door and let them in—tunes I'd never heard,
Mozart maybe, or Bach,
> then something out of some Romany songbook.

Once, though, late, I marched up to bitch—
room darkened in candlelight,
> stench of wine and stale cigars,
then peeking around the door, a bearded turnip—middle-aged, balding,
rimless bifocals balanced on his nose.

A flower, a bottle. A portable typewriter on a little pine table
candled like a shrine,
and edging that candlelight a room of ragged books—Swedenborg,
Dante, *The Tibetan Book of the Dead.*

Steppenwolf in Macon? Playing Mozart on the mandolin?

Ah, the music of the spheres, the old pawnbroker quipped,

                                       or maybe *that* was misery.
And what a grim Jeremiah the memory turns out to be, dragging
its sack of ashes
                out toward the edges of eternity, spilling an irony here,
a tragedy there, when what we need most often
is a simple psalm.

Out of the woods behind my chair
                               a hiker drags onto the path, old guy sagging
in sweatshirt and gym shorts. He nods, huffing, gawking
at the mandolin, which chirps right on with
its garbled melody,
                  picked up now by the mockingbird across the cove.

Down the path he waddles and vanishes into the trees.
Adiós, chimes the mandolin,
                  ciao, adieu.

Every tune's a farewell, says my friend Steve Belew,
a lament, a dirge, a requiem . . .

Then what does the memory have up its sleeve?
What does it mean to do
                        with that man upstairs and his ladybug mandolin?
Those mournful baroque notes?

Or this picture I've kept of him alone,
near dusk,
       at a kitchen table wobbling on a short leg, his elbow tipping
a bottle to a glass
          as he stutter-counts like a man
half-dopey for sleep the houseflies crawling his cabinets and dishes,
his crusted cans of sardines and chili,
                  to discover, finally,
how this might go on forever, all time darkening
into a stained light
shattered by the window, unless . . .

Clink and slow gurgle—
            neck of bottle, lip of glass—
and the greasy walls tilting their greasy tulips this way and that as the chair
slides an inch, the table rocks,
and a misbehaving elbow
            knocks the mandolin to the floor . . .
Listen. Creak of the chair
as the soul leans out toward the open window. How many times already
has it pitched its little tirade
of abandonment?
        Little soul, says Epictetus, *bearing about a corpse.*

And how stubborn it seems now, and impersonal,
pigheaded, pitiless.
        Not the would-be corpse, no,
sodden with booze and slouching already on the windowsill,
but the cocked revolver rising in its palm.

Viper thoughts, viper thoughts, a phrase I caught from Coleridge . . .
unless there is only the world,

                and after that, the absence of the world.
The mockingbird, and after that, the absence
of the mockingbird. The mandolin . . .

And this endless chirping
across the water—alarm of the spirit or simple praise?

  ~

Across the cove
             the baggy geezer in gym shorts stumbles out of the trees.
He parts the branches and sits
on the weedy bank. On the green water his reflection is lost
in the reflection of trees. Legs crossed,
he stares at a sunken limb struggling out of the water.

Wind riffles the water and doesn't disturb him. The jay in the thicket
doesn't disturb him,
            or the rowdy mandolin,
or the mockingbird, or the single crow high in sun-glare.

How still he sits, legs crossed, staring. Who knows what music
he's listening to now? Who knows
but he's succeeded finally in renouncing the world
and is listening this moment to Jesus
              or Buddha?

And who knows if he sees the low branch bobbing, the shadow pouring
itself into the water,
            the moccasin, black as a tree root, glistening,
its beauty a witness to the world's sense of irony?

Along the jagged bank it plows a subtle
but quivering wake. Watch out, bullfrog. Watch out, philosopher.

HOMAGE TO BUCK CLINE

At the edge of town,
past Landers' Rexall Drugstore, the road whipped right then hard downhill
over the tracks of the L&N Railroad,
                                and one night in '65,
stoned on a glass of Mateus rosé with spaghetti
homemade by my girlfriend's mother,
                                I gunned it for the thrill of the dip,
and peeled a little rubber coming back to the road . . .

Up ahead the river, the Etowah,
                                and the buttery glaze the moon spread
across the concrete railing of the bridge,
then the traffic light at the corner of the North Canton Store,
where sour Buck Cline
                        sat in his dark patrol car with the gold badge
of the Canton Police stenciled on his door,
                                waiting for some Romeo,
Don Juan, some small-town Lothario, to run the light
in his father's Impala . . .

Yes, so much relies on the imagination . . .

and what troubles he mulled
                        those tedious midnights, wrangling in
the rowdies, the would-be toughs
circling the Burger Chef
                        in their jacked-up street rods.

✦

And imagination, of course, depends on so much . . .

Take the polished memory of my grandfather's horse barn
with its hayloft full of jewels,
                        or the pasture and the riding ring, the dog lots

full of beagles, the swaybacked chicken houses crawling
with mice,
                    with cockroaches, slugs, with maggots of the dream-life . . .

Or Mr. Cantrell on the floor of his South Canton greenhouse,
his hands churning clods in the glazed filth.
I remember, yes,
                    the good rose requires good filth.

So you'd drive by slowly under the green signal and give Buck a nod,
and maybe in the dark cab an eye would flare,
                                        or not,
having come to what he'd come to in middle age, making
his poor living
                    out-toughing the tough.

⚓

Call it perverse, Poe would,
                            that heady surge of folly that clobbered me
at the light as my foot revved and lifted and the V-8 squalled
under the jumping hood.

What else to say about that rush
                            in my heart as I caught Buck Cline
looking up from his clipboard in the dark car backed into shadows . . .

then the light going green
                            and me pulling out, turning left,
and the long slope of highway past the Burger Chef stretching out
like a drag strip under the stars . . .
Perverse, truly.
Three miles from home and a quarter-mile lead, and I floored it, barking
off some Firestone for the Burger Chef crowd,
                                        forty-five, fifty-five,
and Buck growing smaller in my rearview,
eighty no sweat, and who-knows-what at the top of the hill,

nothing on me but darkness
                          and the curve past the rock barn,
the straightaway sloping toward the South Canton bridge,

nothing but the darkness my headlights butchered,
then tiny in my mirror
                    those blue lights throbbing . . .

⁓

Had the stars ever been so frazzled
and on fire, there on the shoulder of Highway 5 with our headlights killed
and the towered lights of the Pony League ballpark
long gone black,
                    only two small taillights far behind and fading?

Crickets and a rush of wind
                          and under the bridge, the river rounding
the big flat rock where Ace, the shoeblack at the Canton Barber Shop,
fished on Sundays in his ratty straw hat,
then the light in my face
                    and the growl behind it . . .
Shut up, he'd ask the questions . . .
                              And did,
glaring over the beam of his flashlight at the license I'd had for a month.

"You been drinking, boy? Didn't see me back there?"
"No, sir. No, sir," and over the trees
beyond the river,
                    the stars flared and calmed and flared again
as he glanced from the license to my face and back,
breathing my name twice, or my father's . . .

"Reckon your daddy'd like to get you out of jail?"
"No, sir." "No, sir" to everything,
and the dizzy stars
                    flaring again over the hazy trees,

the river jeering where the big flat rock jutted under the shadowy bridge
and deep under the current

               the blue catfish wallowed the mud . . .

Something divine in the memory:

all those dusty little windows of the brain opening inward,
a mirror inside a mirror

                       inside a mirror. *Glimpse Into Eternity,* read the sign
at the Cherokee High School Science Fair,
and when you leaned into the peephole of the big black box
taller than your head,

              somehow your eyes kept going and going . . .

Once in a theater line in Marietta, Georgia, an old saw from my hometown
shaved off some conversation.

                 Sunday evening, early nineties,
and across the square lush with dogwoods
the bells of the First Baptist chimed

               an old hymn, far off, but loud enough
to bend him closer.

Something about his eyes I've remembered,
pale, but sharp,

          the streetlight under the bleached stars catching them
in that gleam of deep reverie—like the eyes of a scientist,
or a saint,

       when the clouds finally open . . .

"Your old man," he said, "you should've seen him play football,"
meaning Canton High, 1941,

            the fall before the war.

Everything was in those eyes,
                    and that word he edged toward, the way
he uttered it with such reverence over the church bells,
as if he'd tasted its weight
on his tongue for years, careful for the perfect usage,
that true word that said it all—"Tough."

And stayed tough enough
even after the war
                    when the shrapnel gnawed into the small of his back
with every step he took
up or down the service ramp at Holcomb Chevrolet, every step
he took across the concrete garage
on that splinter of a bone
                              the Japanese navy left in his leg,
that memory always alive and violent, though never spoken,
having in its pain too much of the divine,
                                        the unapproachable . . .

Tough also one night
at Little League when a drunk behind the backstop kept deviling the umpire—
big man in overalls, a mill worker, hard, poor, angry,
all the desperate adjectives,
                              and the words frothing out merciless and ugly,
and the man's own boy at the plate
trying to see the baseball through that rain of curses,
until the umpire, Doyle Fowler, threw off his mask and charged around
the backstop,
              the man, though, the mouth, had picked up a shovel,
and caught him with the blade
square in the face,
                    and my father, out of the dugout, fallen suddenly

on him, the mouth, the drunk,

                                  arms around him in a wrenching hug,

not out of anger, but something else,

and them on the ground,

                         the one man weeping,

and my father talking, not shouting, but talking quietly

and hugging the whipped man harder and harder,

as though he'd known all along

                              a secret the man thought no one knew . . .

Like the generations of leaves,

Homer says, *the lives of mortal men.* Or something close, and that night

whole generations trembled

                         under the nervous stars as Buck Cline,

like a slightly stunted Ajax, leaned down

and speared me in the eyeball with the beam of his flashlight.

"You think you can whip my ass?"

I shook my head.

                     He held out the license like a gift,

"You think you can whip your daddy's ass?"

I shook my head again,

                        looking up where his pocked and shadowed face

blocked the glare of the moon.

Maybe in the long haul,

as a friend says, most everything blows off steadily to the shoulder

of the road and wallows like litter

                        in the dark we leave behind, things

that have disheartened, haunted, obsessed, delighted,

until finally there's nothing to distract us

from that last curve opening

                    onto the homestretch . . .

I agree. To the shoulder of the road, to the shoulder, but always waiting
to fly out of those gullies

               on these sudden and unaccountable gusts . . .

     ~

And so much hangs on it,

                  the way memory toughens us up for that tumble
and drift of eternity, for the unpatrolled landscape
of the psyche unfurling,

             and so much, certainly,
on those unknown connections, far back, we used to credit to the stars . . .

Buck Cline,

          how many charming stars in your crown?
One certainly for the night you spared me
for my father

            on the graveled shoulder of Georgia 5
with the bloody moon's own halo glowing around your head.

Saint Buck, I kept saying all the way home, and lit in an uncluttered niche
of my memory

            a little shrine . . . Saint Buck
of the handy blackjack,
Saint Buck of the billy, of the speed trap, of the dark patrol car lurking
in the shadows,

            troubled patron of would-be toughs,
of war heroes and weeping boys,

street cop, surely, of the City to come . . .

KENNY ROEBUCK'S KNUCKLE-CURVE

Slow and goofy as the kid himself, it rises out of the crowd-noise and memory,
wobbles off the mound in a long jerky float
                                                like the face of drunk
coming out of a bar, luminous under the streetlights,
rising, dipping, weaving,
                           hovering over sidewalk and oily street,
closer, closer, until gradually you see it's a face
you know, a face
you've mourned in the mirror—
                                stitched, battered, scarred—
the very mug of failure, but floating now in hard-won abandon,
lost to the world, recklessly at peace,
easy to swat as a saint,
                        and you rock back, swing,
and it hops, weaves, jerks,
rockets at your crotch, and once again the world isn't what you think,
and the memory, already wobbling, knuckles off
into voices, laughter, jeers,
                        that sobering pop of the catcher's mitt.

VIGILANCE

for Barry Hannah

All morning in the secret place
among the jays and finches biding their time at the feeders,
the cardinals, the towhees,
                          the stray mosquito and the sweat bee,
the pacified Lab with her beef joint
and the long caravan of ants
                          trekking the wilderness of needles and dry grass.

First scent of the Bradford pears and the pink dogwoods opening,
the cherries, the magnolia, all the old magicians
honing their tricks,
                  as the leaves cloud and clear my pages
like the shadows of passing saints . . .

Days now I've pondered
what my mother-in-law calls the Endtime, and the limp millennium,
which has simply rolled over
                          like a grizzled dog in front of a fire,

days now trying to make the Jesus of Mark
jibe with the Gospel of John . . .

~

Meteors last night.

Rocked back in a beach chair in the front yard, I watched them
scratch across the black sky.
                  Down the street
the rough grate of skateboards and rollerblades, the smell of meat grilling
over charcoal. A brassy music, something Latin,
drifting off someone's deck . . .

So what was that twinge in the chest? Hope, distress?
All this searching for the Kingdom of God . . .

Out there or in here
is what I need to know, whether those capacious taunting celestials
are only pointless sizzles, or if one, maybe,
inconspicuous, faint as a pinhead,

                  is a blue Parousia unfolding.

A neighbor of mine has a sticker on the bumper of his pickup—
It there hadn't been a Pearl Harbor,

                 there wouldn't have been a Hiroshima,

which, he swears, has something to do with the signs, with hymn
and holy trumpet sweeping across the cosmos.
Perhaps, though, somewhere

                in the dark matter of history, a synapse
or two has shorted-out. Spark and sizzle,
spark and sizzle . . .

How to stitch together those loose connections?
So much stress on the needle-bone of faith . . .

He's a quiet man, my neighbor, who fights in his garden
a low-tech battle with ruin,

            hand hoe, spade, garbage bag . . .

I'm fairly low-tech also, believing
that the old truths are never old-fashioned,

               believing they just show up
each season in a fresh cut, a new fabric—sandals and robe
or flip-flops and jersey.

I watch and wait,
follow the common recipe for vigilance. Yes, *if the goodman of the house
had known in what watch the thief would come* . . .

~

One night in a cancer ward
in Oxford, Mississippi,
                        Jesus appeared to my friend Barry Hannah.
I've neglected you, Barry said, and Jesus,
a tall man, barrel-chested, nodded quietly, or simply stared—
I've forgotten the whole story.

He told me this on a patio in Sewanee, Tennessee,
and because of his face
I wasn't surprised to hear it spoken so casually between a swig from a shake
and the lighting of a cigarette,
                    because of his face, I think,
still glassy from the chemo, like the face
of a man come home from a war, not tired exactly,
                             or anything
I'd call fearful, more the face of a man who's discovered in his scars
something terrible, or something holy.

~

Which put me in mind of my father-in-law
on his paper route
                in northwest Montana. Icy night and stars like silver neon,
mountains dropping to valley and the occasional paper tube
leaning out of the emptiness . . .
                      Suddenly in the headlights of his truck
Jesus standing on the shoulder of the road.

He came home weeping.
He staggered out of the kitchen, spilling his coffee, struggling
to describe those strange eyes, that glazed face,

not tired exactly, or afraid,
but more like someone stunned, or hurt,
the face of a man
who's seen in his wounds something terrible . . .

꒰ꜛ꒱

These are the blessed, yes, the fortunate witnesses, the ever-abiding,
who have found in their rucksacks
enough to tide them over,
while I too often perch
among the scribes and Pharisees, flustered with argument,

or rail like Flannery's poor Misfit, frayed
and wrathful, drawing down
on the grandmother
his beautifully empirical resurrection theology—

It ain't right I wasn't there . . . if I had of been there
I would of known . . .

꒰ꜛ꒱

And though I scratch my head profoundly,
I cherish also the smaller witnesses
and hold under my cap the conjectures of Mr. Emerson
who divines among the daily
a necessity in spirit
to manifest itself in material forms . . .

Thus once or twice a year we see Him in the clouds.
A picture crops up off UPI, a storm churning the edge of a California desert.
And, yes, if you turn it just so
a face comes out in the wallow
of shadow and light. Or someone in Chicago or Philly
has caught again in the evening glare off a high rise
a suspiciously holy profile.

Yes, accolades also to the minor mystics

                                   who spiritualize the world's minutiae.
Like my neighbor again who grew a yellow rose
wilted with the sign of the cross, or his sister in Biloxi
who once saw the Virgin swimming
in a bowl of vegetable soup.

                          Accolades, yes, to Ramona Barreras
of Phoenix, Arizona, who pulled from her oven in 1977
a tortilla scorched with the face of Christ,
which may or may not

                     have been the face that appeared
some ten years later in Bras d'Or
on an outside wall of a Tim Hortons Restaurant,
though both made the papers

                        and drew their share of pilgrims.

꙳

Spouts portly Mr. Blake, *every thing that lives is holy!*

Which any backsliding Hindu could tell you . . .

But what does it mean that God keeps stamping his image on pastry
and French toast,

                 on biscuits lightly burned around the edges?

꙳

Once my mother-in-law dreamed
she was floating down a river on an outhouse. True. The water rushing
in through a half-moon window,

                        wild buck and kick of the current,
then somewhere up ahead, in fog
and darkness, the prodigious rush of a waterfall . . .

It was not the Jordan, she says, but claims it still as a sign.
Who knows?

I listen in the dream and in the world. I watch
and wait, turning over rose petals,

                          scrutinizing taco shells, piecrusts,
these constantly mutating faces in the clouds
gathering now

             in their own dark way over the suburb.

~

Wind-gust and a sprinkle of rain, and such a strong scent of pear tree
and cherry whipping across the yard,

                     it feels like the world
has re-upped on its lease.

Such a drawn-out and low-key unraveling of the sorrows—
small earthquakes in California, a mudslide in Mexico,
famine, yes, but always famine,

                  and the hundreds of little wars flagging up
and firing out . . .

And these centuries of slowly accruing misery?
Vigilance, I say. Vigilance and virtue, or what we can muster—
and the moon will not give its light, and the stars
will fall from the sky.

Yes, says the old woman, stirring her cocoa,
If the owner of the outhouse

                had known when the river would flood . . .

MELVILLE IN THE BASS BOAT

. . . meditation and water are wedded for ever.

Three hours I drifted the black cove, throwing deep runners, live shiners,
rattle-bugs and jigs,
                    a Vienna sausage, a pickle,
a mustard-soaked sardine, and for all my stealth and trickery,
failed to conjure
one small mystery caged in the bones of a fish.

                                     Never mind,
there was a book in the bottom of the boat, a paperback, slightly soggy,
and I propped the rod and primed the lantern.
                              Over the oily lake
the stars burned only a little dimmer, though soon
I glowed in a buoy of light.

Wind off the open water, and wave-slap. Boat-drift then
and the tiny *Pequod,* fat-sailed,
                        "plunged like fate into the lone Atlantic."

Sizzle of crickets, cicadas harping from the far pines,
and occasionally out of that directionless dark,
                            one curious owl quizzing
those nameless voices of the cove.

Over the blending rhythms of water and word,
over "that deep, blue, bottomless soul,"
                        how easily the mind drifts . . .

Then spark and slap of the dream-fish, leaping far out, like a thought,
and the felt vibration in the nerve,

                    that trembling to know, to take
another crack at whatever might surface—that mind-flash,
that "ungraspable phantom of life,"
                    that bony metaphor.

III

FIRST WOODS

Bump and jostle, the road falling fast into rut, ditch, washout,
pines cuffing the windows, and me in the cab
a constant bounce between my old man and my uncle
as we bring up the tail
of a caravan of trucks tumbling like a rockslide
leveling into splash and creek-bog,
then back-end swerve and up, and rear tires throwing mud
as my old man crunches gears in a field of orange light
where the sun falls in layers
through the splayed tops of pines . . .

and here we are on my uncle's place,
tailgates dropping, cages
swinging open, the meadow of brown grass crazy with scent,
until one bark rises, circles and leads,
and the whole pack swarms the woods.

Buzzards over the field, and crows, then a circus of bats,

but mostly I've kept the jar and pitch, a clearing of cut hay,
the moonlight rusting a tractor, and off
in the black woods, that thing I never saw, dragging
those frantic voices.

VIOLETS

Little wallow of snuff pouching her lower lip, my grandmother spits
into a marble flower box
                    and tilts a wide sprinkle from a rusted watering can.

Already this morning, August like a sweaty blanket grates the skin,
and the little African violets speckling
the narrow porch boxes
                    gore up purple in the heavy light.
1955, and my grandmother isn't old, though she stoops at the shoulders
and treads what she calls the shady side of the slope.
She shuffles from box to box, leaning over violets, spitting into the black silk
a clotted stream of tobacco juice.
                    Hex? Nutrient?
Slayer of aphids and mealybugs?

Not then, but now, I think of her desperate faith in dirt,
the prudence of watering can, the balance
of light and shade.
                    Her name was Lily, and she dreamed of flowers.
Little cousins of the dream flowers,
she called her violets. Other dreams she never shared.

She spit tobacco juice into her flower boxes
and wiped her mouth on her sleeve—
                    a small mouth, wrinkled,
blackened around the edges like a wilting leaf.

AFTER THE STROKE

By the time he'd hit eighty, he was something out of Ovid,
his long beak thin and hooked,
                                the fingers of one hand curled and stiff.
Still, he never flew. Only sat in his lawn chair by the highway,
waving a bum wing at passing cars.

I was a timid kid, easily spooked. And it seemed like touchy gods
were everywhere—in the horns
and roar of diesels, in thunder, wind, tree limbs thrashing
the windows at night.

I was ashamed to be afraid of my grandfather.
But the hair on his ears!
                        The cackle in his throat!
Then on his birthday, my mother coaxed me into the yard.
I carried the cake with the one tiny candle

and sat it on a towel in the shade.
I tried not to tremble,
but it felt like gods were everywhere—in the grimy clouds
smothering the pine tops, the chainsaw
in Cantrell's woods—everywhere, everywhere,
and from the look of the man
in the lawn chair, he'd pissed one off.

A SWIPE OF SLICK'S HOOK

Eyes blackened, lip bleeding, he crossed the highway
in front of my grandfather's store,
                              a glinting swipe of his nickel hook
warning off the one car passing. A blistering afternoon,
two-minute summer downpour, then the sun steaming the blacktop like a river,

and the way he staggered—one-stepping, flapping wings, dragging
his foot like a Holiness shuffle—it might have been the Jordan
and him some soul desperate for salvation,
or sympathy, or worse still, credit.

Easy enough to see he was plastered.
His wife had left again, or had simply left, I can't remember.
I was only fourteen,
and the heat alone would've made you dizzy.

Skinned eyes and cracked babble,
that VA hook flailing the air—of all the ragged pictures
of grief, I don't know why he'd shadow me,

though something, sure, about the feel of this house, this empty dark,
as though you were holding everything you loved
in a hand that had vanished.

IN SUNDAY SCHOOL

No one ever knew the lesson.
Sunday after Sunday, we sat around a wobbly table

and listened to Mr. Reynolds twist a Southern Baptist slant
into a Bible story none of us had read.

Almost in high school and no one knew the meaning
of the widow's mite, or why the father of the prodigal son

killed the fatted calf. No one understood the parable
of the talents, or could even recite the Ten Commandments.

We were always as blank as the empty blackboard,
sniggering and cracking jokes,

until Mr. Reynolds, one morning, spun midverse
and threw his lesson book at Ricky Doehla.

He stared at his hand, stood, and left the room.
That may have been the morning we all grew up.

And having grown up eventually left home,
left Canton, left the church

to be gutted into a new City Hall,
where the commandments that count

are the laws of the state,
though Jesus still lingers in the remodeled lobby—

trapped in stained glass—
breaking into baskets his fishes and loaves.

HOLIDAYS AND SUNDAYS

They'd settle in our living room, cross their legs—three or four uncles,
my old man. They'd stare at each other
and pull at their ears, while the women cleared the dishes.

Okay, maybe somebody would mention rain
and draw a nod from across the room, or a ball game
that had gone into extra innings,

but mostly there was silence, as though they'd all agreed
the world was beyond comment.

I grew up thinking this was how men behaved, holding
their thoughts close to their chests. A compliment, sure, at dinner—
the beans, the potatoes—but that was it.

Nobody fired off a joke, nobody lobbed a war story
over anybody's bow. Not the tiniest pinch
of philosophy, politics, theology.

Only that slow retreat into calculated silence,
which wasn't exactly boredom,
but more the silence you got at church or funerals,

which was the way you faced the sacred, or death,
or that inscrutable laughter from the kitchen.

PINCH-HITTING IN THE PLAYOFFS

for Ernest Suarez

On the Cherokee High School baseball team, I didn't nab much respect
for being well-read. All the real jocks
got the at bats while I warmed the bench, knocking off
Russian novels.

For me that season was heat and dust and the bad light
of dugouts, and out in the glare
a constant scream off the infield, the outfield, the stands,
until one afternoon
in a frenzied croak the coach broke through the noise—
Grab a bat! Grab a bat!

It was nothing as dramatic as a tied ball game
or even a squeaker we might pull out—
only a chance to take a swing
in a game we had no chance of winning.

I don't even recall the score, only the chatter,
the haze, the heat, the dust
like cannon smoke drifting off the infield,
then the coach against the dugout fence,
shooting crazy signs with his hand—cap, nose, eye,
cap, nose, eye.

And all I could think
was Lev Nikolaevich, don't let Prince Andrei die.

MY DAUGHTER WORKS THE HEAVY BAG

A bow to the instructor,
then fighting stance, and the only girl in karate class faces the heavy bag.
Small for fifth grade—*willowlike,* says her mother—
sweaty hair tangled like blown willow branches.

The boys try to ignore her. They fidget against the wall, smirk,
practice their routine of huff and feint.
                                        Circle, barks the instructor,
jab, circle, kick, and the black bag wobbles on its chain.

Again and again, the bony jewels of her fist
                                        jab out in glistening precision,
her flawless legs remember *arabesque* and *glissade.*
Kick, jab, kick, and the bag coughs rhythmically from its gut.

The boys fidget and wait—
then a whisper somewhere, a laugh, a jeer.

She circles the bag—*jab, jab, jab*—flushed, jaw set, huffing
with her punches, huffing with her kicks, circles
to her left and glares.
                        But only at the bag—alone, in herself,
to her own time, in her own rhythm, honing her blocks
and feints, her solitary dance,
having mastered already the first move of self-defense.

A BLESSING, LATE

Up from the creek behind the cul-de-sac, it skulked
through tree line and subdivided shadows, static of crickets
and trembling leaves, following blood
and scent of meat
to leap my backyard fence.

And if I'd tried the window a good second sooner
or hadn't bumped my knee against the blind,
I might have caught it edged
against the shrubbery,
and met it, for a moment, eye to solid eye,
but as it occurred only that gray and long-legged blur
ghosting into the trees.

And I remembered a girl across our street, taping
a poster to a Stop sign. For weeks
pets had been vanishing, the Persian next door, a calico,
even the fat Pomeranian
that prissed behind
my neighbor's invisible fence.

But I kept staring over my blackened shrubs
and wheelbarrow, my stacked bales
of pine-straw, into the dark between the trees, trying
to bring back that glimpse
and trembling, that nervy blur
that suffered no need
for my dog chow, my water bowl,
or my blessing.

LITTLE DREAM OF SPILT COFFEE

for Kelly

Yipes, I thought, *don't put that cup on the floor . . .*
But you'd set it already on the Oriental rug

to pat down the pillows on the sofa,
and of course, when you turned, you caught it with your heel.

My heart, wobbly for days, tipped again
until I saw the cup had turned over but the coffee hadn't spilled—

no, the coffee had stayed in the cup, no mess, no stain,
the shade-grown coffee from Costa Rica still inside the cup,

inexplicable as mysticism, or love, as though the laws of nature
had shifted to accommodate our mistakes.

It was our red cup, I remember, covered with moons
and caribou, and when I picked it up

and held it between us, you steadied it in both hands,
then lifted it to your lips.

STRIPED BANGLE ON SOPE CREEK

I pushed back the branch
                          and it fell like a bracelet across my arm—
a scarlet king or a coral, but panic like beauty
stunned me, and I couldn't remember which pattern was deadly,
the yellow bands against the red,
                          or the red against the black . . .

then a jolt in my head and a blur, and an old poem
opened onto a grave
where gray bones tangled like roots
and a bracelet of black hair circled a wrist bone.
I stood on that path
and felt down my own bones a thrill I couldn't account for,
like my hand paralyzed in the air
or the shadows of the trees having crossed the path . . .

Wind startled the dogwoods, and my arm shook, and shook again,
until the thing wrapped around it
tumbled onto a rock.
Then an odd thought came—black hair or bright?—

as the snake crawled off into leafy shadows, sluggish,
undisturbed, nudging
its black nose through the scrub.

A WALK TO SOPE CREEK

Sometimes when I've made the mistake of anger, which sometimes
breeds the mistake of cruelty, I walk

down the rocky slope above the ruined mill on Sope Creek
where sweet gum and hickory weave sunlight

into gauzy screens. And sometimes when I've made the mistake
of cruelty, which always breeds grief,

I remember how, years ago, my uncle led me, a boy,
into a thicket of pines and taught me to kneel

beside a white stone, the way a man had taught him, a boy,
to pray behind a clapboard church.

Sometimes when my heart is as dark as a stone, I weave
between trees above that crumbling mill

and stumble through those threaded screens of light,
the way an anger must fall

through many stages of remorse.
Any rock, he allowed, can be an altar.

LOVE AT THE SUNSHINE CLUB

Macon, Georgia, 1970

Bloody smear across the moon
and I'm pondering again the sucker punch that decked me at the Shine—
Forsyth Street, forty years ago.
Two bikers, the bartender, me, and to light the fuse
a skinny girl in skintight blue jeans

                    casually humping the jukebox.

I'd just turned to see who was screaming—when bam,
a flash of head-stars!

               Blood in gushes
and a delicate haze screening the dingy lightbulb.
The floor tilted and rolled back,
a bar stool hit the wall, then
circling above me those raw eyes flushed with booze . . .

Tonight in Macon, only a sober and lonely tedium—
a bruised moon we've made
too much of, a few icy stars drifting
across the interstate.

But as long as I remember that wrenched and scalded face,
those shoulders trembling
like a wet dog, that spittle and sweat,
that red fist choking a beer can, how could I ever stop
believing in love?

LEARNING TO BECOME NOTHING

for Carl Hays

Drizzle this morning,
but a cool glare in the brain, and I'm staggering again down Cherry Street
toward that cratered-out joint on Broadway
where one happy night, eons ago, I cut a rug with a hopped-up redhead.

Nothing came of that, Carl, except a few short hours of inexplicable joy,
so that each bad tooth in her gorgeous smile
                                        hardened into a little gem of memory.

Gems, Carl, gems. And this whole street paved with them—Otis Redding
strutting into your jewelry store, a sunburst off
the cracked face of his watch,
                            or that saintly Pearly Brown, blind as the future,
pounding the sidewalk, slashing out a sermon on his National Steel.
God love a cheerful giver, Carl.

Yes, sir. His sign caught the whole shebang—
and now that we're learning to become nothing, we have to learn
to give it all away—every radiance,
every gem—
            cheerful, as you say, being the enigma.

MY POETRY PROFESSOR'S ASHES

remembering Lem Norrell

All those rhetorical contraptions of the metaphysicals
prying us loose from the world!
                              And those licentious exhortations to squeeze the day!
Something about the Anglican burial
brought those back, and with them your voice rousing those metaphors off the page.
It's not like I didn't get a heads-up, right?

But I'd never seen a man's ashes, the human dust, fine, gray,
and when the priest upended the urn
and shook yours into the grass, I thought how much they looked like chalk dust,
like a lifetime of notes erased from a blackboard,
which seemed right enough
                              given what we are and what words come to.

OLD MAN AND NEIGHBORHOOD HAWK

Vague silhouette, like an idea
forming, then a shiver on the pine branch and the hawk takes shape.

It props against twilight to scrutinize the yard, the hedges
and flower beds smudged into gray pools.

My old man, elbow on his walker, stares from a kitchen chair.

The hawk rolls his head, probes hedge, patio, monkey grass,
rhododendrons heavy with black blossoms, trellis of roses.

The old man noses the window, his caught breath clouding the pane.

Something has grabbed an eye, some old impulse
trembling down the nerves. On the bar of the walker his hand trembles.

Then a dive from the branch, a bursting under brush,
and up the hawk rises on wing-slashes, pine-straw, flurry of leaves—

over lawn, fence, street, dragging through streetlight
something pale and squirming—

and my old man's hand flapping toward the window
falls again to his knee.

MY OLD MAN LOVES MY TRUCK

Sometimes when I've driven the twenty-four miles
to buy a few groceries or change a light,

my old man leans on his walker in the doorway of the kitchen
and gazes across the carport at my truck.

And sometimes when the trembling is too much,
he edges his walker over the stoop and inches onto the driveway.

My old man loves my truck. It has all the right dents and scratches,
just the proper amount of rust.

He'll inch around the fenders, checking out the bed and hitch,
he'll ask to pop the hood.

And sometimes when my old man studies the cab, you can hear
in his pocket the empty rattle of keys.

Then his smile goes slack, his jaw flexes.
And soon that nervous rattle of walker, that rattle of bones

as he plows around the fenders at double-speed, checking
the panels, checking the spare,

as though every loss, every letdown, might be cleared up
by thumbing a scratch or kicking a tire.

MY OLD MAN LOVES FRIED OKRA

My old man's tired. He tries to follow the small talk of the woman
who's brought dinner, but his head nods toward his chest.

My old man won't say so, but he's beat, sapped, worn-out.
He tries to track the talk of the woman from his church,

but her words fall out of the air like sick birds,
and his eyelids grow heavy, and his head nods toward his chest.

This woman, this kind woman from Heritage Baptist,
has brought fried chicken, potatoes, a bowl of fried okra.

My old man loves fried okra—the smell of it, the taste of it,
the slight crunch between the teeth.

He eats it at lunchtime, at dinner. Hot from the pan,
cold from the fridge. He eats it with his fingers, like popcorn.

But his eyelids droop again and his head drops slowly
until his elbow slips off the arm of his chair.

This is what frightens me. How can he be too tired for thanks,
too tired to lift his head for the one simple word

he'd want to say? How can he be too tired for okra?

MY FATHER'S GARBAGE CAN

My old man rings me on my cell. The garbage can is beside the road
and needs to be rolled back into the carport.

I scratch my head at the urgency in his voice.

The garbage can is sitting empty beside the road—
it needs to be rolled back into the carport.

How to say, how to say to my father, I can't drive fifty miles
to wheel his garbage can down the driveway?

But I know this isn't my old man asking. His voice, sure,
his gargle and rasp, but not my old man asking.

He knows the miles and the afternoon traffic,
how the big trucks clot the interstate.

His gargle, yes, his rasp and stutter, but not my father.
He knows the miles, he knows the traffic.

This is loneliness, the loose tongue of loneliness
nagging by the window

where he's sat all day with his elbow on his walker, staring
at the oak shade staining the yard

and the garbage can, empty, on the shoulder of the road.

A CHAT WITH MY FATHER

Sometimes when my old man tries to talk, his mind runs like a small boy
on a path through the woods.

You know the story. There's home to get to and it's getting late,
only a little light still slicing through the trees.

And the boy has walked the path so many times
he thinks he can do it in his sleep. But no. Some bird sounds off

way back in the woods, and he tries to ignore it, but it harps again,
and suddenly he's off the path, deeper and deeper

into the trees, wading the shadows, following the strangest
and most beautiful birdsong he's ever heard

until he crosses a stream and catches in the corner of his eye
a ruby as big as his fist, sure, a ruby or some rock

just as precious, and bends to pick it up when a wild dog . . .
no, not a dog, when a wolf barks across a gully,

and he's beating his way through brush and briar, trailing
those barks and howls already fading

in the distance. All the while the woods have grown dark,
and suddenly he looks across the table,

and you see in his eyes that he's lost.

TEDIUM

Every night my old man inches his walker across the kitchen floor—
to the cabinet for a glass, the sink for water.

And usually while he's leaning on the counter, or turning
from the sink with a glass in his hand,

the grandpa clock goes off in the hall. Eight chimes
like a gong falling down a well.

Then it's back through the den, around the sofa, down the hall—
glass wedged into the basket of his walker.

A hand on the bedpost for balance, the cautious lifting of the glass.
A shuffle then down the edge of the bed.

Finally, on the night table a glass of tepid water. A hell of a fuss,
he says, for what only makes him piss.

In the morning on the night table
an empty glass. And beside it a ring in the dust.

MY FATHER ADJUSTS HIS HEARING AIDS

Once again my old man has gutted his hearing aids.
On the table beside him, around the smallest blade of his pocket knife,

his hearing aids lie scattered like the scrutinized guts of bugs.
Somewhere in those parts—the coils, the disks,

the blue copper veins—somewhere in that chaos lies the riddle
of sound. Now in the dark kitchen he faces the window

where the first stars tremble in the branches of his oaks.
The house is as quiet as a broken watch.

He's pieced the clues—nothing will ever be
repaired again, nothing will ever work as it did. The dumb wind

says as much, and the needles raining in the yard.
The silence around his shoulder is my mother's arm.

MY FATHER'S LEFT HAND

Sometimes my old man's hand flutters over his knee, flaps in crazy circles,
and falls back to his leg.

Sometimes it leans for an hour on that bony ledge.

And sometimes when my old man tries to speak, his hand waggles in the air,
chasing a word, then perches again

on the bar of his walker or the arm of a chair.

Sometimes when evening closes down his window and rain blackens
into ice on the sill, it trembles like a sparrow in a storm.

Then full dark falls, and it trembles less, and less, until it's still.

ON CANTRELL'S POND

1

When I was a boy there was a pond behind our house

that eventually filled up with construction runoff—
a muddy pond of stunted catfish,
a mosquito hole, fetid,
wallow and paradise for copperheads, rats, moccasins, frogs,
and no few turtles that could take off your finger
with one surgical snap,

and at night, year-round, the stench rose thick
and seeped in waves
through the cracks in my window
where I'd curl like a snail at the foot of my bed, drifting
on deep breaths, far back.

I'm always dreaming my way back to water:

to a washed-out logging road
plunging to a river
where high buzzards recon the kudzued pines,
to a cove on a lake of monster gar, a tumbling creek
of killer rocks, a sky-black swamp choked with cypress
where I wade out knee-deep with my rod and rattle-bug
and never, in my exhaustion, outrun
the cottonmouth

that blesses my heel with its flower.

2

Why all of this middle-aged noise about getting back?

Though, for sure, in the mornings the leafy banks rustled
with birds—
                    blue jays and cardinals, a towhee or two,
robins, thrashers, and dozens of barn sparrows
mobbing the dam where our neighbor, Mr. Cantrell,
crumbled biscuits for his fish,

and in the summer the forest of sunflowers
nodding in the wind at the edge
of his garden,
and the rosebushes crawling the bank
from the brush dam to his toolshed
all the way up to the chicken house collapsed
in a thicket of briars.

3

But out here, in middle age, or a mile or two beyond,
why all this hubbub about beginnings?
And why only one brief dream
of that pond
when now there's no other way back?

Or only a way back to kudzu and concrete,
to a Kentucky Fried Chicken where our house once stood,
a Taco Bell, a Pizza Hut,
an oily gas station, and across the highway
a Kmart strip mall, a Waffle House
where my grandpa once grazed horses.

In my dream the sky was a loose tumble of charcoal,
the silky trees bare and trembling.
Tall grass bit my ankles. I lifted my feet,
I had someplace to go. Then brush stalks shivered
as I stepped off the bank
and began to walk, carefully,
not on water but on the parched bed
of an empty pond
cobbled entirely with turtles.

CAMPFIRE IN A LIGHT RAIN

1

Out here near the end, sometimes in my despair, I pack
a tent into the truck bed,
a few camping tools, firewood and kindling to save me some trouble,
and sandwiches, of course, and sardines,
water, soda, whatever,

and sometimes drive east to the Oconee River
to sit all night in a folding chair,
feeding sticks into a fire.

No radio, no cell phone, but a battery lantern for books.

Even at the end, I still need books, though the crickets are witness
that the story goes on a little while longer,
and the mallards skiing in
at twilight to bob under a sunken tree,
and the hermit owl far back in the woods
tossing out his eerie vibe,
and the tree frogs in the pines above the riverbank,
and the pines in the wind
above the riverbank.

2

My granny used to hear voices from her childhood,
the voices of schoolchildren
in Pickens County
long shoveled over in sanctified clay.

She never told anyone for fear of being shut away,
but took them as testimony
for that *land beyond the river, that Canaan of the saved.*

You tell me what the end looks like to you,
and I'll tell you about a river
under a night sky,
about the stars guttering out, one by one,
while a thicket of scrub pine darkens into a wall.

Does anyone have another idea?

3

The charred logs sizzle in the rain, and the chill off the river
bores like a dull blade into my knees.
By the time my old man
was my age he could hardly move without a groan.

I sit under the tent flap
and watch the mallards dabble around the fallen oak,
and a few wood ducks, an egret.
Three geese took off an hour ago, stringing out north
over the logging road, and everything now
is settling toward nightfall.

Whatever happened to the promise of wisdom?

The gray beard came, the cracked teeth,
the vanishing hair, the trembling hand,
but what became
of Solomon's crown?

I toss a few more sticks into the fire
and ponder my foolishness—

all of this time searching for purity
and never grasping the nature of ashes.

A HERON ON THE OCONEE

1

Now on the Oconee, on this shallow elbow of quiet water,

the first moist sunlight seeps through the thicket,
and a heron streaked in feathered light strides out among the rocks.

Ruffled and muddy, it wobbles out into the river
and balances on sticks among the rocks,

utterly motionless among the rocks.

2

Near the end, the way my old man stared into the distance,

the way he leaned from his armchair
toward a window, elbow quivering on his walker,

and gazed through oak branches into a broken sky,
is the way this heron, ruffled, muddy,

stares downriver at the water rippling into the trees.

AN ABSENCE

Near the end, only one thing matters.

Yes, it has something to do with the moon and the way
the moon balances so nervously

on the ridge of the barn. This is the landscape of my childhood—
my grandfather's country store, his barn, his pasture.

His chicken houses are already falling, but near the end
only the one thing matters.

It has to do with the prudence of his woods,
the way the trembling needles prove the wind.

Let's sit here by the fence
and watch for the fox that comes each night to the pasture.

Imagine how the moon cools the water in the cow pond.
Yes, things happen in the cool white spaces,

those moments you turn your head—
the way the trembling branch suggests the owl,

or the print by the pond suggests the fox.
Near the end, though, only one thing matters,

and nothing, not even the fox, moves as quietly.

STUDYING THE SMALL HILL

Sometimes when my wife and daughter are asleep
I stumble outside
with our dog at three or four in the morning to piss in the yard.
In winter the moon scorches the tree branches,
and in summer it frosts the hillside
with a shabby glaze.

Then the bird feeders standing in the smudged shadows
of the maples
look like human skulls impaled on poles—
and sometimes wind and crickets and tree frogs
make lurid voices in the trees.

This is when I empty myself of anger and resentment,
and listen to them puddle
in the grass at my feet.

Jack runs the fence line and trots out
of the shadows, panting, to piss in the grass beside me.
Often in his eyes there is more to envy
than anything human,
and gauging the frantic influence
of the moon, I study the small hill bleeding shadows.
It's easy then to affirm the Christ metaphor
and all the tenuous ways
tenderness seeps into the world.

SLOW NIGHTS IN THE BASS BOAT

Some nights when the fishing slows,
when the stripers
and hybrids drift through the cove like elusive thoughts,
you crank in the jig, prop the rod in the boat.

Some nights the trees on the bank are black and soundless,
a fat wall of darkness,
and the silence on the water feels like the voice
of a great absence.

Across the wide cove the lights of the bait shop
flicker like insects,
and, finally, a few stars struggle through the shredded clouds.

Silence, then, exceeds the darkness. Silence.

You grasp the gunwales and lean forward,
you catch a long breath.
That gnawing in your chest sharpens and spreads.
Your grip tightens.

The rustle in your ear is something grand and awful
straining to announce itself.
Your jaw trembles. Out of your yearning
the silence shapes a name.

QUESTION ON ALLATOONA

The moon was in the sky and on the water at the same time, and the sky
filled with stars. A dock jutted into the cove,

and the banks were heavily wooded and dark, the whole cove sizzling
with small sounds. From out of the woods on the far bank,

an owl called twice, paused, then hooted again.
Beyond the cove the lake widened quickly,

and a mile or more away
lights of the fishing camp flickered on the surface of the lake.

Our tackle box sat closed on the floor of the boat.

Far behind us on the porch of a cabin, a guitar
backed up a mandolin. We listened

instead for the question with no answer,

watched the moon on the water, then the moon in the sky,
and when enough silence had passed,

the frogs let go in great bellows up and down
the edge of the water.

There were no bass in that cove. No lunkers,
not even the pretense of a fish. Nobody even bothered

to untangle the backlashed reel.

BLESSINGS, YELLOW MOUNTAIN

I could have killed the snake.
I had a pistol in my belt, a 9mm, a Smith & Wesson,
accurate, deadly, and I was a good shot.

I could have easily killed the snake.

But Jack and I were walking his turf, walking federal land,
and he coiled so placidly
across the oak root, not even lifting his head
to acknowledge our passing.

I could have killed him with one shot. Nobody
would've heard. We were miles
from the nearest road.
But Jack wasn't even curious, and kept pulling me
up the path, sniffing the ground, lifting
a leg to piss on a stone.

I studied the moccasin for a moment longer—
the fat and terrible muscle of him, his black scales rippling
while a small wind
brushed his back with shadows.

Beautiful, sure, but I thought better of inching closer,
then followed the tug of Jack's leash.
Over the top of the ridge
sunlight sliced in layers through the trees,
and suddenly out of the branch quiver,
an antler moved.

THE GROCER'S TACKLE BOX

Not all dreams need to be realized.
—PATTI SMITH

My obsession with gear
comes from a grandpa who rarely caught a fish

but kept in his tackle box one of every lure
he ever sold in his store.

I was especially drawn to the potbellied Bombers,
deep runners meant for pike and walleye,

but also the rainbow Rattlebugs, the pink doll flies trailing
yellow boas
loved by crappie and bass,

and the speckled plastic worms,
rubber frogs and tadpoles, the fat, tangerine Hula Poppers.

He kept his tackle box behind his cash register, tucked
behind cartons of bills and tax receipts.

As a boy I could walk by the Coke box and feel its draw.

Someday, he kept saying, he'd take me fishing
but never did. That was okay.

To prove the promise sometimes outweighs the fish,

he'd often let me open that box and thumb
the barbs on those lures.

A PANIC OF BATS

Near evening I carry a folding chair into the plush shade
of the secret place
and sit facing the house

and the bat box hanging from the guest-room gable.

A quiet breeze in the leaf shelter
as they rise from the box and flit like ashes out of a bonfire,
black, black, black, rising

and flitting like ashes. My gaze flies
with them across the fence
and over the side yard, the way I followed, years ago, the ashes

of a burning house, little black wings drifting
over the wavy panic
of children crowding an upstairs window,

drifting across the hillside, rising and rising, falling
and falling and falling
onto the backs of grazing horses,
into the tall grass of my grandfather's pasture.

SUMMER, 1968

We'd watch the news on my portable Philco.
The jungle was black and white. The bodies were black and white.

The whole house strained in its silence. I was 1-A.

One night my old man threw an alarm clock across my room.
He screamed something, but all I caught

was a cheap alarm clock, the size of a softball, ringing in the wallboard.

The screen flickered. The jungle snowed gray, the bodies gray.
The alarm clock, stuck in the wallboard, rang

for a minute or more. Nobody touched it for days.

BRING THE BEAUTIFUL HORSES

Some days nothing helps.

Some days not even a basket of apples will bring the black horses
out of the past,

and Christ Pantocrator
seems little more than the face of an absurd hippie.

(My old man bent toward the gaping mouth. He sniffed, it was confirmed.
Nothing would help.)

Some days the sweetest words will not bring a blessing from the sky,
or sweeten the breakfast table with a smile,

or bring the beautiful horses out of the magical past.

(Nobody knew death like my father—
the Solomons, Wake Island, Guadalcanal. Thirty years

prepping bodies in a funeral home.) Some days on the prayer porch
the petitions never clear the trees,

and there is nothing to do but rock
and watch the wind rattle the maples and pin oaks.

(When he turned toward my aunt and shook his head,
everyone knew it was accomplished.)

Some days those beautiful horses will not leave the shadows
of their hill.

Some days nothing helps.

HUBERT BLANKENSHIP

Needing credit, he edges through the heavy door, head down,
and quietly closes the screen behind him.

This is Blankenship, father of five, owner of a plow horse and a cow.

Out of habit he leans against the counter by the stove.
He pats the pockets of his overalls

for the grocery list penciled on a torn paper bag,
then rolls into a strip of newsprint

the last of his Prince Albert.
He hardly takes his eyes off his boot, sliced on one side

to accommodate his bunion, and hands
the list to my grandfather. Bull of the Woods, three tins

of sardines, Spam, peanut butter, two loaves of bread (Colonial),
then back to the musty feed room

where he ignores the hand truck leaning against the wall

and hefts onto his shoulder a hundred-pound bag of horse feed.
He rises to full height, snorting

but hardly burdened,
and parades, head high, to the bed of his pickup.

FOUL BALL

The river was off-limits, but occasionally a foul ball would fly back

over the press box, over the narrow drive
and down the hill,

and there we were—where what we called the ballpark rock
jutted into the Etowah.

On hot nights the stench would make you gag.

Two miles below the rendering plant
and chicken parts still flooded up in the pool beyond the rock—
clots of dirty feathers, feet,

an occasional head with glazed eyes wide.
We'd hold our noses and try to breathe through our mouths.

Once, though, the smell was too much
and we had to give it up.

Listen, it wasn't what you think. It was only Little League,
and they gave you free ice cream

for retrieving a foul. No, we weren't overcome
by thoughts of filth, disease,
or fish kills. We were running down a long hill, dodging

trees and undergrowth, trying
to find a ball before it found the river.

A NERVOUS BOY

1

I was a nervous boy, small and nervous.
I liked to hide.

I sought out places of refuge—
close spaces where thick air was a balm for remorse.

And there were many secret places
between the store and the dog lots, the barn and ball field.

The chicken house, for instance, at the top of the path
to my grandfather's dog lots,
empty for years
but still rich with the smell of broilers and feed—

a quiet dark enjoyed by rats
and rat snakes, spiders, roaches, beetles, earwigs,

and once, a stray dog birthing her litter in the dank sawdust.

One day I hid there all afternoon.

2

I hadn't wanted to shoot the rabbit.
It sat on a ridge of the pasture, stiff ears reaching for the sky,

and even from that distance I could see it trembling.
Wind whipped the grass and blew in
the stench of dog turds. My stomach turned.

My grandfather laid the barrel of his rifle on a fence rail
and held the stock to my shoulder.
I was a good shot. I sighted the head, I steadied,

but I didn't want to shoot that rabbit trembling
in perpetual surrender. I inched high, squeezed, and dirt flew up
a foot beyond it.

My grandfather sighed as though my failure
suggested the sort of man I'd be.
But I didn't want to shoot that rabbit.

He shrugged. He shook his head.
He pumped the rifle again
and pressed the stock tight against my shoulder.

3

From the chicken house
I could hear the horse neighing in his stall,
the crows in the pines on the hill above the dog lots.

After a while, shouts rose from the ball field at the foot of the hill.
But I only wanted to hide.

I only wanted the dark, the solitude.

I don't recall the shot or the rabbit jumping
sideways and falling,
only that old man lifting it by the ears

and flinging it into the dog lot.
I must've shot the rabbit.

A SMALL REMEMBRANCE

... I have learned the impossibility of avoiding surrender.
—ANDRE DUBUS

1

Beside a Coleman tent,
beside a lake, I light a small fire of damp sticks and twigs.

The flames struggle to catch in the kindling.
Smoke billows and blows away.

Across the lake a coyote wails (or a stray dog).
Then wind again in the trees.

A doctor I knew once
told me that every time he watched a patient die
he thought he could see something tangible

leaving the body. He didn't say soul,
but I knew what he meant.

Surely the soul billows and blows away.

Tonight I light a small fire
of remembrance, a small fire by a still lake,
in a light drizzle. The month is November,
though the night isn't cold.

Smoke billows and blows away.

Memory also, I fear,
the features of a face, the sound of a voice,
a typical phrase.

2

When I can't reach my daughter, or my wife,
and the black flower
of anxiety blooms in my chest and chokes off my breath,

I try to think of my father, years ago, away at war
in the oily water of the Pacific,
the black jungles of Florida Island and Guadalcanal.

I try to imagine the darkness blooming
in the chest of his father,
his mother on her prayer bones at bedside,

their anxiety as they hover over their radio, twisting dials,
desperate for war news,

the static of radio, wind, and whispered plea,
which makes my worry small.

3

Some mornings on the prayer porch
with the brown eyes of Christ Pantocrater gazing at me
from Kelly's icon,

I pray for the coyote den in the woods
beyond the cul-de-sac.

I pray to be like the coyote, wary and full of craft,
fully aware of the moment
and only the moment,

praying urgently to the moon and the trees
and the steel wind hacking through the scrub brush.

Who wouldn't want to know what she knows?
That is, what she knows
and nothing more?

4

Landscapes plowed over, paved over, prayed over,
live only in memory.

My grandfather's house and grocery,

his field and barn, our house of green shingles beside

the highway, the homemade infield
where my old man hit grounders and taught the subtleties
of the double play—

how many memories are left
for them to live in? If I stand in that Kmart parking lot, trying
to take bearings—the store must have sat here,

my grandfather's house there,
the barn behind me (somewhere), our house

down the highway—no dice.
The pasture graded and paved, lined with paint for parking cars,

all's a vague approximation.

5

Clouds roll and the rain picks up.
The lake is black.
I squint and gaze back years across the black water.

A spotlight beams out of the darkness and strikes
the superstructure of the ship.

Six gun turrets swivel to shoot it out.

Soon barrels flash all across the horizon—
thunder and fire—

the water itself on fire.

In the lifeboat someone asked
about the pain.
                    (Only his right hand
kept his intestines from spilling into the boat.)

A little sting, he said, from the salt water.

6

I remember my grandmother's cedar chest,
the rich smell of the kept
and sacred—

crocheted bedspread folded in plastic, hand-stitched quilts,
the wooden box of battle ribbons, the purple cameo
shaped like a heart.

The profile out of history.

A small boy shouldn't be trusted with such things.

7

Beside this cabin tent,
beside this lake, I light a small fire of damp sticks and twigs.

Clouds shred. Smokes billows slightly
and blows away. The coyote (or stray dog)
prays loudly to the moon.

The breath tries to catch in my chest.

Who survived two years
in a San Diego hospital came home to leave
many memories,
though the soul will finally billow and blow away.

And memory.

Smoke off a damp fire.

CATHEDRALS

1

Near nightfall, in summer, an owl would plague the scrub woods
beyond Cantrell's pond.

Or a mourning dove, hard to tell. (Question or lament,
question or lament?)

Branches slapped the roof and sides of the tree house.
Light fell
in thin slices through the oak

and dimmed away in the shadows. The woods beyond the pond
dimmed away, then the pond,
then the yard.
                    Spiders took to their corners,
roaches to their corners. Traffic thinned slowly on the highway.

Then the screech owl would startle the scrub woods.

Soon someone else would call, someone from the house.
But I'd not answer. Not yet. I liked to hide.
I liked to sit alone in the dark.

No one knew where to find me. Still,
if I held my breath for a moment, if I stayed quiet, if I listened
and didn't breathe,

a wind might rise and garble my name.

2

You could hardly breathe.

In a corner of the hayloft, where a thin ray of light
from a grimy window fell once a day
in midafternoon

and drew across the loft a quivering veil of dust,
you became almost breathless.

Behind a few tattered hay bales
and moldy bags of oats,
you could, in those days, feel a credible silence.
(Careful, though! The feed chutes!)

One Sunday, when I was a boy,
my uncle took me there and draped his jacket
across a sturdy bale.

We used it as a pew, and the prayer he spoke rose
and faded into the rafters.
He lifted a finger to his lips, as if to say *Listen*.

(Silence is the language of faith.) Suddenly, at that sign,

no whistling through windows
of horse stalls, no rasping of floor boards, no worry
of crossbeams propping up rafters and roof.

3

A deep green cave of branches. A leafy darkness.
Something waiting to be born?

I'd sit beside the trunk and gaze up. On clear days patches
of blue ragged
through the upper branches. (Enough to make a sailor's suit?)

In a light rain the green leaves sparkled,
and once I found a glossy snake skin draped
in a low fork.

But at Christmas the branches sparkled with electric bulbs—
red, green, and blue
and the yellow of traffic lights. My father climbed a ladder
and strung them all the way to the top.

Taller than the house, with leaves as wide
as a small boy's head, cones
as large as footballs.

I was a small, nervous boy.
I liked to hide
and nurture my prayers in dusty places.

Under the skirts
of my grandmother's magnolia, a gentleness set in.

A gentleness
is all I knew to call it, a calm, a solitude.

DRESS BLUES

Bad luck, he believed, to throw away a Bible. So a small stack
moldered on a table in the basement—

a pocket New Testament with Psalms and Proverbs, a gilded King James
in a red leather jacket, an Oxford Revised Standard,

a Tyndale's New Testament. (Where did he get that?)
I walked down one morning to find his leather-bound Masonic

at the bottom of the stack,
which brought back those evenings

he'd come home late, his jacket smelling of stale tobacco,
and on his breath a sweetness

it took me years to recognize. What mysteries were revealed
those late nights in the windowless lodge

he never revealed to me. At his funeral the Grand Master stood
at the grave and challenged us

to change our lives. (Someday we'd be lying in his place.)
Two sailors in dress blues

folded the flag that had covered the casket
while a third stood off and bugled taps—solemn, mournful, lovely.

Weeks later, I learned it was a recording,
but still recalled
that glint of sunlight as the bugle touched his lips.

EYE TO EYE

Suddenly I noticed the silence—the robins, jays, mockingbirds
all gone quiet, the cardinals and song sparrows quiet.

Then as Jack and I turned onto the homeward loop of our walk,
the sky startled us with a shriek—

two hawks circling above the pines, screaming from tree to tree,
two hawks from the heavy nest

above our neighbor's house, screaming then going silent
in the branches of a Bradford pear.

We crossed under that tree and stopped to catch
the larger hawk, the female, eye to eye.

Jack sat by the curb and stared. I stared.
And head cocked, leaning forward, she stared, incredulous,

working her jaw, quietly, nervously.
I made faces, snarled, bared my teeth, and the hawk

never flinched. Only stared until those orange inflamed eyes
became the terrible jaundiced eyes of my father

that final moment he raised his lids.
(The silenced voice tells the truth.)

Like my father's jaw, her jaw trembled.

SPRING, 2012

I rub my eyes. The world is still green—
a lime dust coating the porch tiles, rocking chairs, patio, yard,

delicate as a mourning veil.

A green finch dances between the bird feeders.
I can't breathe, my eyes water. My friend can't breathe either.

She's lost her son to an IED. No details yet. Routine patrol
around a dusty village far away.

Tea waits on the table between us, and two blueberry scones.
Impossible, of course, to talk about loneliness

or vague aspirations. Rain today, then a cooling.
In a week or so, dogwoods flowering along the back fence.

After that, maple sap staining the hoods of our cars.

KELLY SLEEPING

Sometimes when she sleeps, her face against the pillow (or sheet)
almost achieves an otherworldly peace.

Sometimes when the traffic and bother of the day dissolve
and her deeper self eases out, when sunlight edges

through curtains and drapes the bed, I know she's in another place,
a purer place, which perhaps doesn't include me,

though certainly includes love, which may include the possibility of me.
Sometimes then her face against the sheet (or pillow)

achieves (almost) an otherworldly calm (do I dare say that?)
and glows (almost) as it glowed years ago

just after our daughter's head slipped through the birth canal.

I remember that wet sticky swirl of hair
turning slightly so the slick body might follow more easily,

and how the midwife or nurse or doctor (or someone)
laid an firm open hand under that head

and guided our child into the world.
When that hand laid our daughter on her mother's breast,

such a sigh followed, a long

exhausted breath, and (stunned) I saw in my wife's face
an ecstasy I knew I'd never (quite) see again.

AN OLD ENEMY

Just past midnight when I walked out back to piss in the yard

I saw at my feet
in a patch of moonlight

the old enemy coiled on the root of a cherry tree.

It didn't rattle or move, and I thought it might be dead,
then the fat tail twitched
as a slight wind washed the root with shadows.

I backed away slowly, looking for the shovel
I kept leaning against the fence.

It wasn't there. So thinking *omen,* I left the snake
and walked back into the house.

This morning I saw my mistake. A rope the tree trimmers
left last week
lay draped across the root of the cherry.

Omen? Maybe. But no mistake.

In deep memory the danger remains—
the fat rope
coiled and ready to strike.

LITTLE KING SNAKE ON THE PRAYER PORCH

Wanting to live, it had wedged itself between a porch rail
and the screen and hung there

as Jack barked and backed up and lunged forward
and barked again.

An Eastern king snake, jelly-black
with buttery stripes. Beautiful, yes, but slightly common.

Harmless, basically, a constrictor
good for eating rats and other vermin, also an eater

of rattlesnakes and moccasins.
Benevolent, basically,

though it tried to bite when I raked it with a stick.
I steered it toward the door

and watched it sidle across the grass
and thought of a time I would have taken more joy

in its appearance, would have felt it
to be something miraculous,

a necklace, say, fallen from a witch's neck,
suddenly come alive

and slithering into the brush.

SUNDOWN SYNDROME

The last night my mother spent in Kennestone Hospital
my cell rang at four,
her voice raw and pleading—the nurses were trying to kill her,
I needed to phone the police.

Around that voice my bedroom tilted.

Nurses were wheeling everyone into the basement.
Thus all those hysterical gurneys clacking
down the hall. Nothing would convince her otherwise—

watch the elevators, listen
to the screams. No one damned to the basement
ever comes back.

Last evening, fifty geese circled chaotically
above our backyard pines, then vaguely fell into a V
to break up and flag again.

Something had gone haywire,
shorted-out in the nervous circuitry
of the world—dozens of Canada geese reeling

over the suburb, tumbling, wheeling, ragging-out
in a Babel of figure eights. A full two minutes
before the planet leveled

and sharp black lines
arrowed south over pine tops not quite dark.

MY MOTHER'S ABSCESS

The receptionist, in her marbled booth, jabs a pink nail into the phone.
All day, maybe, she hasn't noticed the potted ficus
between the revolving doors.

The potted ficus! Maybe no one has noticed but me
with my brown-bagged Dewar's and my fat Russian novel, on my way
to the second-floor waiting room
where, a few rooms down, surgeons are slicing a loop
from my mother's colon.

A snake in the ficus tree? Sure, as though it had slithered
out of some patient's dream, a red snake curled
like a bowel around the ficus, little red snake like something
out of a trick shop, curled
around the skinny trunk of the ficus.

When I was a kid I saw omens everywhere—a crow on the mailbox,
a black cat at a ball game, that evil number
turning up on Fridays . . .
                              I scratch my beard.
Upstairs my mother lies drugged, beyond dreams, beyond signs,
and here I'm spooked by the tiniest snake?

A few leaves tremble, the body loops. The lewd head rises
like a little chip off the original nightmare.

REHAB

In 308 my mother is stewing. Not because a nurse smashed
her porcelain vase and scattered roses across the floor,

or because an aide swiped an apple salvaged from her lunch tray.

Even now from this bed, she feels dust invading her house,
glazing her china cabinet, wind whistling

under the plate-glass door in the den. The chill circles her kitchen.

The furnace is off, the house trembling. The bony clock creaks
in the shifting corner. Leaves swirl in the garage.

In 308 my mother broods, her cracked ribs are slow to mend.

She lies on her back, hands at her side, jaw set,
staring at the ceiling, at the blistered ceiling,

as though what she studies

are answers written in a secret code
and not just water stains under a light fixture.

ARRIVAL AT RIVERSTONE

Only a sparrow, she said. But I thought its song was lovely.

Then we went inside. People greeted us
and smiled, but none was my father. You could see

that in her face. Strangers all.
They shuffled behind walkers and canes, pointing

out the dining hall, the craft hall, the oversized flat-screen
for weekend movies. We trudged down the corridor

past the rec room where an old man leaning on a pool table
used his cane as a cue. Room 515. Last on the left.

Her name was misspelled on the door. She grumbled in.

Her bed was there, a dresser, two tables, her TV attached
to the cable, a few photos hung "to warm things up."

This place is full of old people, she said.
"A short period of adjustment is not uncommon,"

meaning nothing would be quite as it should.
The place was hot. I crossed the room to crack the window.

Ten feet away a small nest balanced
in the limbs of a dogwood. All she had to do was look.

YOUNG NURSE, VA HOSPITAL, 1945

Innocence, perhaps,
caused her to gasp and hold that memory for seventy years:

her leaning against the desk at the nurses' station,
going over meds
with the head nurse,

then a young sailor rolling up in a wheelchair.
Can they give him something
for his pain? His legs and feet are killing him.

She looks down at his scarred face,
his narrow shoulders wrapped in a khaki shawl,
his hands folded in his lap, then . . .

But I always knew what was coming, even the first time
I heard the story. Her grimace tipped me off.

And each time the story was repeated—
often three times in one visit—

I chalked it up to senility.

Now looking over the house
with only a stick or two of mildewed furniture,
the sagging deck, the ragged yard,
the downed fence,

I see that story clearly as an explanation—

the two bandaged stumps
a warning against the pain of absence.

THE MOON MY MOTHER SHOT FOR

She aspired. Yes, she aspired.

But where in Canton, Georgia, could she wear the full-length mink
and the two-carat diamond she scraped

for twenty years to buy? Society
gathered at the country club and pool, the nine-hole golf course.

(My father, neither lawyer nor doctor, never played golf.)

And the twelve settings
of crystal that gathered dust for years in her china cabinet?

No one ever ate sherbet at our house.

All those lovely nights
when the full moon hung like a ballroom chandelier

over the used-car lot across the highway, that mink hung
wrapped in a sheet in their bedroom closet

and the diamond dulled quietly in its velvet box
in a vault at the Etowah Bank.

MAYBE A LITTLE MUSIC

for Mike Mattison

Clearly the door to old age has opened.

Turns out it's the door to the prayer porch, swung wide, inviting me
to the rocking chair, the ceiling fan,

Christ Pantocrator hanging from his post between
panels of porch screen. Nothing to do here

but wait for something to happen. Somewhere else, most likely.
(When my old man lost his job

he went to bed and never got up.) Bird feeders empty
and nattering blue jays wondering

why the buffet's closed. Off in the neighborhood the growl
of leaf blowers and chain saw. Somewhere

a yard fanatic is butchering another tree.
This is what they call the blues, sans guitar and mouth harp.

Maybe a little music would help.

What to do but walk through the door and wait?

OTHERWORLD, UNDERWORLD, PRAYER PORCH

Maybe I'll rise from the dead.

Or live as a shadow. Or maybe I'll never leave you. At Emeritus
an old man plowing the hallway

with a three-wheeled walker
stopped me and grinned, *My goal is to live forever—so far, so good.*

Maybe we never get enough birdsong,
or watery soup
and over-steamed veggies. Still, from the prayer porch
eternity sometimes looks like a raw deal.

Eternal leaf blower and Weedwacker?

(A few days before he died my old man asked about the yard.)
Mostly blue jays at the feeder this morning, rude

and rowdy, and a few cardinals dripping off the trees
like the bloody tears of Christ.

Maybe we rise again only to the good things—honeysuckle,
robins, mockingbirds, doves,
fireflies toward evening, and along the back fence

the steady harping of tree frogs.
On the prayer porch, among the icons, such fancy notions.

OTHER EVIDENCE

Rain now, heavy, and in a few hours
an icy mix, then snow after sundown, heavy, with gusting winds.

The weather guys are rarely wrong.

No milk on the grocery shelves, no bread,
no cornflakes. Certainly I'll regret not splitting more firewood.

Atlanta at a standstill—big rigs abandoned
on the interstate, cars spun out on the shoulders of the roads,

men and women trudging in the snow.

For years now
I've feared the tall pine leaning toward the house,

the loosening soil and the loud crash through the roof.
In the morning, sure, a kind of beauty—

the white blanket draping the yard,
Jack chasing the apple core I throw into the woods,

but also those strange tracks crossing
the yard, skirting the windows

and fading again into the trees.

A SCRAWNY FOX

Near the end, only one thing matters.

Yes, it has something to do with the moon and the way
the moon balances so nervously

on the rooftops of neighborhood houses. You remember the landscape
of your childhood, your house and yard,

the yards and houses of your friends. Near the end, though,
only one thing matters.

Maybe there was a wood where you played,
and that wood is gone now, paved over for parking cars.

At night, before sleep, it comes to you again—
your longing for the wilderness, the fox you saw last week

at the end of your cul-de-sac. Maybe you put out dog chow
and wait, at night, on your back porch.

Maybe you tire and close your eyes. Things happen
when you close your eyes—an owl leaves a branch trembling,

the dog food disappears. You'd love to see that fox again.
Near the end, though, only one thing matters,

and nothing, not even the fox, moves as quietly.

ACKNOWLEDGMENTS

David Bottoms, poems from *Armored Hearts: Selected and New Poems, Vagrant Grace, Waltzing through the Endtime, We Almost Disappear,* and *Otherworld, Underworld, Prayer Porch* are copyright © 1995, 1999, 2004, 2004, 2011, and 2018 by David Bottoms. Reprinted with the permission of The Permissions Company, LLC, on behalf of Copper Canyon Press, coppercanyonpress.org. All rights reserved.

From *Armored Hearts: Selected and New Poems* (1995): "Wrestling Angels," "Shooting Rats at the Bibb County Dump," "Below Freezing on Pinelog Mountain," "A Trucker Drives Through His Lost Youth," "Stumptown Attends the Picture Show," "Jamming with the Band at the VFW," "Writing on Napkins at the Sunshine Club," "Calling Across Water at Lion Country Safari," "Rest at the Mercy House," "A Home Buyer Watches the Moon," "Sign for My Father, Who Stressed the Bunt," "Under the Boathouse," "The Copperhead," "In a Jon Boat During a Florida Dawn," "In a U-Haul North of Damascus," "In the Ice Pasture," "Homage to Lester Flatt," "Under the Vulture-Tree," "Naval Photograph: 25 October 1942: What the Hand May Be Saying," "The Anniversary," "The Desk," "Armored Hearts," "In a Kitchen, Late," "Last Nickel Ranch: Plains, Montana," "Hard Easter, Northwest Montana," "A Daughter's Fever," "My Perfect Night," and "Allatoona Evening."

From *Vagrant Grace* (1999): "Night Strategies," "Country Store and Moment of Grace," "A Canoe," and "At the Grave of Martha Ellis."

From *Waltzing through the Endtime* (2004): "Easter Shoes Epistle," "O Mandolin, *O Magnum Mysterium,*" "Homage to Buck Cline," "Kenny Roebuck's Knuckle-Curve," "Melville in the Bass Boat," and "Vigilance."

*   *   *

From *We Almost Disappear* (2011): "First Woods," "Violets," "After the Stroke," "A Swipe of Slick's Hook," "In Sunday School," "Holidays and Sundays," "Pinch-Hitting in the Playoffs," "My Daughter Works the Heavy Bag," "A Blessing, Late," "Little Dream of Spilt Coffee," "A Walk to Sope Creek," "Striped Bangle on Sope Creek," "Love at the Sunshine Club," "Learning to Become Nothing," "My Poetry Professor's Ashes," "Old Man and Neighborhood Hawk," "My Old Man Loves My Truck," "My Old Man Loves Fried Okra," "My Father's Garbage Can," "A Chat with My Father," "Tedium," "My Father Adjusts His Hearing Aids," "My Father's Left Hand," "On Cantrell's Pond," "Campfire in a Light Rain," and "A Heron on the Oconee."

From *Otherworld, Underworld, Prayer Porch* (2018): "An Absence," "Studying the Small Hill," "Slow Nights in the Bass Boat," "Question on Allatoona," "Blessings, Yellow Mountain," "The Grocer's Tackle Box," "A Panic of Bats," "Summer, 1968," "Bring the Beautiful Horses," "Hubert Blakenship," "Foul Ball," "A Nervous Boy," "A Small Remembrance," "Cathedrals," "Dress Blues," "Eye to Eye," "Spring, 2012," "Kelly Sleeping," "An Old Enemy," "Little King Snake on the Prayer Porch," "Sundown Syndrome," "My Mother's Abscess," "Rehab," "Arrival at Riverstone," "Young Nurse, VA Hospital, 1945," "The Moon My Mother Shot For," "Maybe a Little Music," "Otherworld, Underworld, Prayer Porch," "Other Evidence," and "A Scrawny Fox."

David Bottoms would like to thank Kelly Beard, Dave Smith, Ernest Suarez, and Laurie Watel for their friendship, insights, and support. Thanks especially to Vernette Miller for her prayers and encouragement.

DAVID BOTTOMS was the author of nine books of poems, two novels, and a book of essays and interviews. Among the many awards he received for his poetry were the Walt Whitman Award of the Academy of American Poets, an Ingram Merrill Award, an Award in Literature from the American Academy and Institute of Arts and Letters, the Levinson Prize and the Frederick Bock Prize from *Poetry,* and fellowships from the National Endowment for the Arts and the Guggenheim Foundation. He taught at Georgia State University in Atlanta where he held the John B. and Elena Diaz-Verson Amos Distinguished Chair in English Letters. He was the recipient of a Governor's Award in the Arts from the Georgia Humanities Council and he served for twelve years as Poet Laureate of Georgia.

ERNEST SUAREZ is David M. O'Connell Professor of English at the Catholic University of America in Washington, D.C., and the executive director of the Association of Literary Scholars, Critics, and Writers. He has published widely on southern literature, poetry, and music.